The Managed Economy

The Managed Economy

*Papers presented to Section F (Economics)
at the 1969 Annual Meeting of the British
Association for the Advancement of Science*

Edited by Alec Cairncross

BARNES & NOBLE, Inc.

NEW YORK

PUBLISHERS & BOOKSELLERS SINCE 1873

SBN 389 04057 6

First published in the United States, 1970 by Barnes & Noble, Inc.

Printed in Great Britain

Contents

1560244

List of Tables

Introductory Note

The papers in this volume were presented to Section F of the British Association in September 1969 at its Exeter meeting. They deal with problems of economic management, whether in relation to the private sector (as, for example, in Chapter 7), the public sector (as in Chapters 6 and 9), or the economy as a whole (as in the earlier chapters). The discussion ranges over the similarities and differences between national economic management and business management (Chapter 1), the limitations of planning and control in both contexts (Chapter 2), and the degree of convergence between the economic systems of Eastern and Western Europe (Chapter 3). Two papers describe ways in which economic management can be made more sophisticated: on the one hand through the contribution of short-term economic forecasting to the central problems of management and control of the economy (Chapter 4) and on the other through the use of cost-benefit analysis in reaching decisions about capital projects (Chapter 8). Two other papers concentrate on instruments of control over the economy: either general control through monetary weapons so as to improve economic stability (Chapter 5) or direct intervention by the Government to alter market structure in the interests of industrial efficiency (Chapter 7). The part played by subordinate authorities is discussed in relation to the nationalised industries in Chapter 6 and to the growth of local authority expenditure in Chapter 9.

The papers collected here are not intended to serve as a comprehensive guide to the problems of modern economic management. No single volume, and certainly not one of this brevity, could make any such claim. But they may provide a useful introduction to the mixture of issues—economic, social, political, and administrative (to say nothing of psychological and technological)—involved in the management of an industrial economy. They are offered as fragments of that inchoate subject referred to at the end of my own contribution as " managerial economics " or " economic administration ": a subject which, if it is to be developed, " will have to blend economic theory and decision theory with realistic analysis of the way in which organisations behave and administrative structures become adapted to the pressures on them " (p. 22).

My thanks are due to Carl Sandberg who kindly prepared the Index.

Alec Cairncross

Part I

Management and Planning

1

The Managed Economy

Alec Cairncross

I

Some years after the war I had a discussion with a young Russian in Moscow about the capitalist system and the changes it was under-going. I dwelt on the inadequacy of a term like 'capitalism' as a description of the many different economic systems in Western countries, on the high proportion of profits in Britain that went to the government in tax, on the controls imposed on private industry and its dependence on government policy, on the growth of the public sector and a number of other developments in the role of the state since the days of Marx. My friend was unimpressed. If 'capitalism' was not an adequate description of the British economic system, perhaps I could suggest an alternative label? I must not jib at labels since one word was enough to describe all mankind, viz. humanity. In desperation I suggested 'the welfare state'. This was unconvincing for a different reason—my inability to think of an adequate transla-tion into French, the language in which our discussion took place.

If a similar challenge were issued to me now, I should probably take refuge in a different label—'the managed economy'—and feel the same sense of discomfort derived in equal measure from the inadequacy of the phrase and from the lack of a satisfactory French equivalent. But it is, I suppose, the fashionable answer to the question: 'What have we got in place of capitalism?' just as the fashionable answer used to be: 'the welfare state'. Of course, there remains a school of thought which is not content with either label and is dedicated to economic planning. My Russian friend, for example, would still be likely to argue that 'the planned economy', however it may be evolving, is fundamentally different from anything that we have ever had here.

* Master of St Peter's College, Oxford, and President of Section F, 1968/69.

It is worth reflecting a little on these labels and what they signify. The welfare state is fundamentally egalitarian in concept. It grew out of the emergence to political power of the working class, the idea of a common minimum below which living standards should not be allowed to fall, and the need to make collective provision for health, education and old age. It rested heavily on taxation as an instrument for the finance of such collective provision as well as for the redistribution of income or at least for the concentration of fiscal burdens on the broadest shoulders. But it did not, as such, imply any particular system of state control or ownership of industry.

The first objective of a managed economy, on the other hand, was originally stability. It grew out of the heavy unemployment experienced between the wars, the ideas associated with the name of Keynes, and the greater weight of government activity in relation to the size of the economy. In course of time other objectives have been brought under the heading of management, notably faster growth, a more even distribution of income, and a wider diffusion of economic development over the country. But the initial emphasis was on the need to maintain uninterrupted full employment.

It is possible to argue that there is no essential difference between a managed economy and a planned economy, and that planning is simply a rather inflexible form of management. This would mean that we now live in a planned economy without the courage to describe it correctly. But there are, I believe, important differences in emphasis which amount to a difference in principle.

For example, the keynote of planning is certainly not stabilisation. There may have been Keynesian overtones to planning even in the thirties but historically it was associated either with war-time control or with the efforts of the U.S.S.R. to industrialise her economy—the antithesis, surely, of stabilisation and for that matter a better example of an economy out of control than of one in course of planned development. Nobody would pretend today that those who decided on the first Five-Year Plan foresaw all its consequences and deliberately accepted the sacrifices involved. As so often in later years 'planning' was little more than camouflage for an investment boom and the inflation and controls that went with it.

It is arguable that the difference between planning and management lies in concern for growth rather than stability. Even this is not quite true, or at least not in Britain. For example, in three early and influential discussions of planning by British economists,

Professor Meade's *Planning and the Price Mechanism*, Sir Arthur Lewis' *Principles of Economic Planning* and Evan Durbin's *The Politics of Democratic Socialism*, there is either no mention of economic growth or it is largely disregarded or thought to be not particularly affected by planning.[1] But none of these writers was a believer in long-term planning *à la russe* and they could more accurately be listed as supporters of economic management. Where the argument for planning is in dynamic terms it generally does rest explicitly or implicitly on the view that growth will benefit.

The fact is that those who think of planning as something different from management usually have a longer time-dimension in mind. They are thinking not of what can be done to influence economic activity or the distribution of income over the next year or two but how to bring about a transformation of the economy either in the form of industrialisation or of some drastic structural change that would have continuing effects on efficiency and output. Second, they are thinking more of direct intervention to influence production than of attempts to manage demand without detailed intervention. And finally, they usually have in mind a system of tighter central control or at least a closer linkage between the plans of individual enterprises and the plans of the central government.

Broadly speaking, therefore, the situation in Britain is that management is linked with the ideas of stabilisation, the short-run and control of aggregate demand, while planning is associated with growth, the long-run and structural change in industry and elsewhere. Management, to put it succinctly, is primarily the affair of the Treasury, while planning is (or was in 1969) the responsibility of the Department of Economic Affairs.

II

A generation or so ago no one would have claimed that the economy was managed. Public debate hardly touched on the question how the economy should be run even when the existing system was being denounced root and branch. The defenders of the system, although willing to consider detailed improvements calling for government intervention, regarded it as fundamentally self-regulating. The more radical critics, attacking the private ownership of the means of production, gave little thought to the organisation of the economy

[1] Devons, E (1965) 'Planning and economic growth', *Scott. J. Polit. Econ.,* **12,** 105.

under socialism: what was to follow capitalism could be worked out after it had disappeared. Within the government it is hardly too much to say that economic policy in its modern sense of 'policy towards the economy as a whole' did not exist. There was little or no discussion of measures to promote economic stability or growth; most of the Budget—in the first two decades of this century at least—went in paying for wars—past, present and future; and the major issues of a macro-economic character tended to centre round the distribution of income.

The term 'management' came in with the ideas of Keynes for currency management. It was already in common use in this context in the early twenties and when the *Treatise on Money* appeared in 1930 it not only featured in the heading of Book VII—*The Management of Money*—but in the title to each of the eight ensuing chapters. When pre-war economists spoke of 'management' they were thinking almost exclusively of monetary policy and of the greater stability of prices and activity that might follow the sagacious use of monetary policy. When the argument broadened to include the use of budgetary measures for the same purpose, it tended to be conducted in terms of 'management of demand'. The emphasis was essentially on the regulation of demand, and on the elimination of cyclical fluctuations. Management was thus seen as concerned primarily with stabilisation policy and with the short-run, since stability is by definition a short-term affair. The management of the economy in this sense inevitably rested with the Treasury because the Budget, monetary policy and other instruments of demand management were already the responsibility of the Treasury.

But management, as now practised, had other and quite different origins. The emergence of the welfare state enormously extended the scope of government and brought about not only a large increase in public expenditure on health, education and housing, but also an equally formidable increase in social security benefits, pensions, family allowances, grants and transfer payments of all kinds. At the same time, the nationalisation of a large sector of industry brought formally under public control what previously had been part of the private sector in form if rarely in substance.

The growth of the public sector in these various ways posed problems of management of a more immediate kind. In a country where one man in four is employed by a public authority, public investment exceeds private investment, and the combined expenditure of all public authorities (including the capital expenditure of the national-ised industries) is over half the size of the national income, there are plenty of management problems to be faced that are at least akin to those facing private industry, although there are also many important differences. Apart from this, the total impact of public authorities on the economy is now too compelling to be neglected in the calculations of private industry and must itself be the subject of management.

Indeed we have moved from a world in which the government played a very subordinate part in economic life to one in which the pronouncements and actions of government are of overwhelming importance to a large sector of industry. The government is expected to take responsibility for almost everything—particularly if things go wrong—and to be correspondingly ready with statements of policy and well-conceived measures on every imaginable occasion.

There is a further reason for the emergence of the managed economy: the growth of big business. The bigger the average size of business unit the more is organised and planned rather than left to the operation of market forces. The possibility of a parallel growth in government planning is suggested almost inevitably by successful business planning; and co-ordination of the activities of large businesses becomes itself an object of government policy.

III

In considering the problems of a managed economy it is well to begin by recognising that management is by no means the same as control. In the strict sense of the term no economy is or can be controlled. This is true even of a command economy just as it is true also of an army: once instructions issued at the centre filter down the line they have to be reinterpreted in the face of local circumstances. In a system like ours where the government has to rely heavily on persuasion, co-operation, and incentives of all kinds it does not even have the illusion of control: the system is specifically devised to respond to pressure from below.

Every economic system is, therefore, a mixture of organisation and free enterprise. All that is open to debate is the strength of the mixture; the optimum degree of organisation and centralised control. At one extreme is complete *laissez-faire* with no one taking conscious thought for the operation of the system and the price mechanism operating as a co-ordinating agency to link together the plans of

individual producers and consumers. At the opposite extreme is a
war economy, organised for one purpose and one only—to win the
war; or a planned economy of the Eastern European type where
organisation for purposes determined by government requires individual preferences to be subordinated although not, of course,
ignored.

The system that we now have lies between these extremes. It is not
a planned economy in the sense that it sets out to supersede the
planning of privately organised firms by obliging them to conform to
aims of policy arrived at independently by the state. But neither is it
one in which the activities of firms are left to be dictated exclusively
by market forces reflecting the preferences of individual producers
and consumers without regard to wider social purposes and longer-
term goals. Business has to keep one eye on the government and what
it will do next. The government sets the framework within which
businesses operate; but it still leaves consumer demand as the
principal motor force governing economic activity.

The market forces that operate have to be rigged by the government since it cannot afford to allow the workings of the economic
system to reflect exclusively—and imperfectly— the spending habits
of individuals in their private capacity, with all the instability, in-
equality and short-sightedness that this would imply. But the government cannot carry the process too far without making the system
insensitive to consumer preferences and wasteful in its use of the
resources necessary to meet these preferences. It cannot set itself up as
the sole judge of what should eventually reach the market or of the
terms on which consumers should be asked to choose between con-
flicting products. Management does not mean control over the
consumer and an end to uncertainty about what he will want: it does
not make foresight redundant or extinguish the risk of error. On the
contrary, it means a greater alertness both to immediate wants as
well as long-run needs, an acceptance of the fact of change from
whatever source it springs, and an effort to turn change to advantage
by preparing for it in advance.

It is not true, therefore—as has sometimes been argued—that
management means giving the consumer an anaesthetic to prevent
him from upsetting somebody's apple-cart. Organisations, large and
small, at the national level and at the level of the individual firm,
have to reckon with market forces that are only partially under
control. Moreover the kind of business organisation that ultimately

triumphs is not settled by direct government action but is also shaped by market forces through a competitive struggle between alternative structures. The more the government is willing to let the consumer influence what is produced, the more it must devolve on business units capable of translating market demand, actual or potential, into effective supply. Where buying decisions are dispersed and independent a greater degree of discretion must be allowed to those in touch with the buyers, and a correspondingly looser degree of control and organisation is appropriate. Except to the extent that monopolistic influences operate in the opposite direction, market forces are a powerful decentralising agency.

At the same time, there are many important needs that cannot be satisfied through the market and positively require centralised decisions, as well as other needs that can be met more cheaply or effectively by collective effort than by private initiative. The margin between collective provision and reliance on the free operation of the market is necessarily a shifting one, depending on the willingness of the public to be taxed, the efficiency of public authorities, the threat to the welfare of others in what one man does or neglects to do, and so on. The balance depends also on popular aspirations since the more firmly the government is expected to promote greater equality, faster growth, a more stable economy, and so on, the more centralised the control necessary to secure those objectives.

The degree of control exerted in the management of the economy is also affected by international factors. We are all familiar with the tendency for balance of payments difficulties to dictate the way in which the economy is managed. These difficulties are the more likely to arise, the more dependent a country is on foreign trade and finance. The greater is that dependence, the stronger is the compulsion to accept less ambitious policy objectives, to give priority to the accumulation of adequate reserves of liquid assets and to working for more effective management of the international economy.

Management does not imply an equal degree of control over decisions of all kinds. There are some matters where a few key decisions have to be taken centrally while in many others it is plainly impossible to do more than influence decisions taken farther down. This is as true of management of the economy as of other kinds of management. For example, the level of aggregate demand depends closely on governmental decisions while the level of demand for individual products (or, still more, individual brands of the same

product) is not so easily controlled; and as a rule it is less necessary—
indeed less desirable—that the government should seek to control it.
Similarly, the government has a greater stake in the division of output
between consumption and investment than in the balance between
different constituents of the two; and the first lends itself more
readily than the second to a decision at the centre.

This reflection brings us back to the link between management and
stabilization policy. The objective of economic stability is one which
can normally be secured by a comparatively small number of far-
reaching decisions by a central authority, all of them within the competence of the authority and calculated to leave subordinate authorities and enterprises free of detailed control. For this purpose it is
enough to have a limited staff of economists, furnished with general
indices of economic activity and performance, and to operate through
budgetary and monetary controls supplemented from time to time by
intervention of a more direct kind. On the other hand, the object of
more rapid economic growth normally requires a very large number
of decisions by the enterprises within which growth takes place and
may not easily be influenced for the better by decisions lying within
the competence of a central authority. The links between centrally-
taken decisions and economic growth are not fully understood by
economists or anyone else, and are certainly open to dispute. At the
same time, the links between decisions at the point of production
or sale and economic growth are usually very obvious if by economic
growth is meant an improvement in efficiency and productivity. It
may be possible to influence these decisions from the centre only by
a series of specific measures involving step-by-step negotiations and
consultations on an extensive scale; and in the process some of the
thrust that normal competitive processes would provide may be
sacrificed so that the net gain in productivity is minimal. Some aims
of policy, therefore, lend themselves less readily to centralised
decision-taking than others; or, to put it more bluntly, are less likely
to be achieved by government action.

IV

I turn next to consider some of the problems posed for economic
analysis by management of the economy. I propose to concentrate on
some of the facts of life about management which economists too
often overlook and to leave on one side those mysteries about the

economy and how it really works which are—or should be—the main preoccupation of economists. In making this distinction, however, I should like to emphasise that the activities of government are themselves part of what we call 'the economy' and that it is increasingly difficult to offer useful explanations of the working of the economy without simultaneously trying to explain the working of its management.

First of all, I should like to stress the importance of purely organisational factors which are common to management at the national level and at the level of the individual enterprise. Thereafter I shall turn to other aspects of management where the similarity is either less striking or non-existent.

Organisational factors are rarely analysed in economic theory, which developed largely in terms of an analysis of market forces generated by bargains between individual consumers and producers. For this purpose consumers and producers alike were treated as independent, self-consistent units and their behaviour was studied almost entirely from outside, apart from assumptions about motivation derived from introspection. Even the theory of the firm, which might be expected to consider what goes on inside business enterprises, was often developed as a series of mathematical theorems with only the most perfunctory references to management. Organisation, if mentioned at all, tended to be confined to those parts of economic theory which dealt with cartels and monopolistic influences reflecting the links between one firm and another; that is, the external, not the internal, relations of the firm.

It was only when economists had to face such questions as: 'What sets a limit to the growth of the firm?' that they found themselves obliged to stress organisational factors. As a rule this question was raised in discussion of the relative merits and survival value of big and small firms. But it is obviously a question that goes to the roots of the whole economic system. For if economists are unable to find in their own discipline of thought any reason why firms cease to grow or any grounds for expecting efficiency to suffer when firms unite, they equally lose the power to find economic arguments against the unification of each industry in turn under public ownership and so in the end unification of the entire industry of the country.

In recent years economists have found themselves taking an increasing interest in management and the domestic problems of running a business and have become more conscious of elements in decision-taking that were previously neglected. Although decision-taking in industry is by no means the same as in government, there are common elements and so far as this is so economists have already begun to address themselves to the problems of the managed economy that flow from the organisational side of management.

Both in industry and in government, management is largely pre-occupied with change: sometimes of its own making, more often arising elsewhere. It is the principal function of management to control and direct change and to develop instruments for this purpose. Whether in reacting to change or in promoting it, however, management has to contend with its own human limitations, notably ignorance, uncertainty and shortage of time.

Any manager finds himself obliged to take decisions on the basis of limited information and in a state of uncertainty about most of the relevant variables. He has a great many decisions to take, often at short notice and under considerable pressure of time. He has also to overcome human friction of all kinds: to consult and inform his colleagues, maintain morale among his subordinates, and keep under review the existing arrangements by which his work is linked with that of others. If any economist proposes to analyse his business and put forward useful theories on the basis of this analysis, he cannot disregard these facts even if he finds it necessary, for some purposes, to abstract from them. Similarly any economist analysing the management of the economy cannot disregard the simple facts of government decision-taking. Decisions do not exist in abstraction from the machinery by which they are arrived at: the machinery imposes its own limitations on the decisions.

(a) Ignorance

Take, for example, the fact of ignorance. No management or government could ever imagine what it would be like to be in a state of perfect information. When a government acts it cannot possibly know with any real confidence what the situation is. It is bound to be out-of-date. Probably it has to rely on second-hand information. This is particularly true of a government using general economic information made up mainly of aggregates and averages compiled at one remove from the primary data. Once quantitative information has been boiled down into statistical indices there is no possibility of verifying it by direct enquiry, and random checks not only take time but may be highly unreliable. It is one of the inescapable facts of life that the more highly centralised the management the more remote are those who have to assess what is happening from first-hand contact with events. Even if the statistics are completely accurate and the best possible measure that could be devised, they do not carry the hints and overtones of what lies behind them that comes from direct communication with individual businesses.

It is common both in business and in government to blame a bad decision on an unnecessary degree of ignorance. This may be entirely justified. But it does not follow that everything would be changed by speeding up the flow of information to the centre. No doubt this would help. But the information available would still be out-of-date; the process of speeding up its collection might be very costly; and very often the trouble lies in the inconsistency of different pieces of information rather than in avoidable lags in collection so that it would still be possible to offer different interpretations of what was really happening, however quickly each item of information came in. Every economic historian knows that long after all the statistics have been published there is plenty of room for debate about the story they tell.

In this respect governments are probably a good deal worse off than individual businesses which have less reason to be in doubt about what is going on under their noses. But I wonder whether large businesses, however efficient, are sure that they know at any point in time just how their capital development is going or how they should weigh a rising trend in some branches against a falling trend in others. The British Government's experience at any rate is that it is often hardest to find out what is happening in the public sector—in the nationalised industries or among the local authorities—over which its control (nominally at least) is more direct.

Knowledge of what is happening does not take the Government very far in deciding what to do in framing an economic policy unless it can make use of some framework into which the facts can be fitted, i.e. unless it has a theory round which to organise the facts. But very often economic theory indicates only the direction that action should take, not the magnitude of the action that is called for. I am told that President Truman expressed disappointment in the post-war years with the advice that he received from economists because he thought that he could decide without their help in what direction he should move and they could proffer no advice on the one thing on which he needed guidance, i.e. by how much to move.

(b) Uncertainty

Coupled with outright ignorance is uncertainty. Managerial decisions are almost always taken in uncertainty not only as to the facts but as to the right interpretation to put on them. 'Everything is uncertain, most of all the future' as Per Jacobson was fond of saying. Theories of managerial behaviour which assume that managers have access to all the relevant facts and are maximising measurable quantities by reference to known relationships are therefore highly misleading. Any decision that is taken involves the risk of error and the main problem is to decide how to run one's risks. Even if a judgment can be shown to have been 'right' in some sense at the time it was taken, it may prove in retrospect to have been wrong because of events that could not have been foreseen or adequately allowed for. It is often more important to be alive to the real range of contingencies and to have that feel for anything that may upset existing trends which we call 'hunch' than to be able to marshal the known variables in the light of established theory. For this purpose it is invaluable to be able to see economic problems in historical perspective or bring to bear on them a long and varied experience of similar past situations.

It seems to me to follow from what I have said that there are severe limits to the value of economic theory to the policy-maker in a managed economy. The main function of theory is to direct attention to the relevant variables, but this does not take us very far if there is no reliable information about the variables (i.e. if we are ignorant) or if the uncertainties governing decision-taking lie outside economics altogether (e.g. in the political field). Economic theory may help us to see what additional information ought to be collected or what information is really material to any specific problem. So far as it throws light on how the economic system really works it greatly reduces the uncertainty involved in government intervention in the working of the system. But once governments themselves are one of the main elements in the system, their behaviour has itself to be encompassed by the theory. This cannot be done by simply adding another variable to existing models and treating governments as if they were no more than the point at which the second differential crossed the x-axis. Indeed it cannot be done by mathematical methods at all since governments do not conform to mathematical rules.

The plain fact is that ignorance, uncertainty and inconsistency make it correspondingly difficult to devise and apply any logical system of wide generality such as can be based on the simple axioms of economic behaviour. We are driven to rely on limited applications to specific situations except where it is possible to arrive at satisfactory explanations that apply in their most general form in the face of human irrationality (e.g. in explaining economic fluctuations).

(c) Time

Next, I would stress the importance of time in economic management. This enters in a number of different ways.

First of all there is the familiar distinction between the short-run and the long. Any act of management has a series of effects over time, some of them quickly apparent, others delayed. It is necessary to visualize all these effects and if, as often happens, some are favourable and others unfavourable, to balance them against one another. The conflict between long-run and short-run considerations is a large subject on which I have little new to say.

It is, however, necessary to emphasise that this conflict is complicated by political and administrative considerations. In democratic society governments have an uncertain length of life and hesitate to curtail it deliberately by giving precedence to long-run gains at the cost of short-term unpopularity. They are to some extent in the same situation as companies exposed to the threat of a takeover in that there is a premium on action conferring clear and immediate benefits.

Economic myopia of this kind does not, however, deter governments from taking large risks with considerable light-heartedness. For they may enter into commitments involving heavy eventual outlays so long as they either win immediate credit or escape from awkward political dilemmas or gratify some critical section of opinion. They may, in other words, accept economic risks for largely non-economic reasons and be tempted to exaggerate the long-term economic benefits or minimise the outlays which they require.

The balancing of short and long term gains is further complicated by the need to devolve responsibility on subordinate authorities within the public sector. Such devolution may involve laying down criteria for public investment based on success in meeting market requirements. The nationalised industries, for example, may find their performances judged in terms of the profits they earn and may be led to neglect forms of expenditure which, although debited as current costs, are justified mainly by their long-run consequences:

for example, expenditure on training, development of new products, improvements in quality, and so on. The solution to this dilemma may lie not, as some economists would instinctively suppose, in refining the criteria laid down from above, but in devising different structures of responsibility so as to leave greater freedom of action coupled with different incentives and a different training for those to whom it is granted.

Time has another and quite different significance in management. It shapes decisions by determining the speed with which they are arrived at. Governments, no less than managements, have to make up their minds quickly on most things. They are expected to comment as soon as a problem becomes apparent to the public and that comment may be expected to foreshadow a policy which in turn commits them to action. They are under constant pressure to provide a full explanation of things only dimly appreciated and say at once what they propose to do as soon as questions are asked. Unlike academic and other commentators, governments cannot usually plead lack of time or the need for prior research before coming to a decision. They may set up a Royal Commission here and there but they cannot put policy-making into commission. They may be reminded of earlier pronouncements, and indeed of their party programme before taking office, but once in power they cannot treat earlier views and promises as Holy Writ or they might as well hand over to the Civil Servants. They have still to work their policies out in the face of new circumstances, changing opinions and unsuspected objections—always under pressure of time.

It is indeed a frequent source of misunderstanding in public affairs that ministers and senior officials never have unlimited time. They are, in fact, harassed men. A Minister's time may be largely hypothecated to trivialities—inescapable engagements and urgent matters of detail—so that high policy has to be squeezed into odd intervals and the small hours; there are always strong temptations merely to react to events without trying to be ahead of them. Yet in government as in business, management practice increasingly involves organisation for the purpose of getting ahead of events. In a sense this is what planning is all about.

An outstanding illustration of this is the preparation of economic forecasts. These are the basis on which business programmes are drawn up and these programmes—of production, sales, investments, etc.—are effectively summaries of the policies of the enterprises concerned. Similarly, in government, the forecasts of GNP and the balance of payments, once they are accepted and provided no fresh action seems called for, are tantamount to plans and can be regarded as embodying government policy. Of course, governments may disregard forecasts or abandon forecasting altogether, particularly if they are conscious that there is a risk of crisis for which forecasts cannot allow and to which improvisation is the only possible response. But so far as the machinery of forecasting is highly developed it provides the most convenient way of exploring contingencies and the best starting point for fresh policy decisions. It helps to turn these decisions into amendments to existing plans and ensures that they are forward-looking and geared to a conscious review of future prospects.

While governments may decide to work on the basis of systematic forecasts they have to face the uncertainties of the immediate future and recognise that these uncertainties tend to multiply the longer the time horizon. It is bad enough not to know the outcome of events already in the offing—whether the Suez Canal will open next year, whether negotiations for joining the Common Market will be successful, whether there will be an exchange crisis, and so on. But in addition there are all the possible events not yet on the horizon—assassination, war, major strikes, etc.—for which it is impossible to provide on any rational basis. Hence although decision-taking may be organised around some form of forecasting, the forecasts will always be taken with a pinch of salt and no amount of economic or any other kind of theory tells us how much salt to add. All that one can say is that economic forecasts extending over a period of several years are necessarily very uncertain and may amount to little more than guesses.

There is also a danger that where policy is arrived at by progressive modification of existing plans, the mechanism of policy-making may become too inflexible. The system of forecasting provides coherence and continuity and makes for timely consideration by everybody concerned since they can see and comment on the outcome expected before anything happens. But the machinery may impose its own rhythm on decision-taking and cause delay or reluctance to take fresh decisions, especially if the forecasts are allowed to exercise a mesmeric effect and are taken seriously in their own right as the shape of things to come instead of as a scaffolding for decision-taking.

The fact that time is not unlimited has other consequences for managerial behaviour. It imposes devolution by busy ministers (whose tenure of office is typically short) just as much as by busy managing directors (who enjoy on the average a much longer tenure). Ministers can take only a limited number of decisions so that others, less politically significant, must be taken by officials. There is a limit to what they can find time to read or (still more) to write; and this means that submissions are usually made to them only when officials feel that they have the whole story or all the arguments to put before them. Ministers run the risk, therefore, that an issue which they might have settled one way has to be settled another because delay has put the first solution out of their power. If they ask: 'Why wasn't I told earlier?' they may find that the answer lies in the large number of other matters that are similarly held up for fear of over-filling their in-trays.

Much the same applies to officials, including those dealing with economic affairs, who are responsible for the continuity of policy. They frequently live in a state of perpetual overload from which there is no obvious escape. Take for example the problem of assimilating information about current economic trends. Anyone seeking to be thoroughly posted on the state of the economy does not lack for material and there is no limit to the amount of time that can be devoted to studying it. It is simply not possible, given the limitations of the human mind, to take on board *all* the known facts, and simultaneously to attend all the committees at which an understanding of the facts may be important, still less to combine these activities with working out in time to influence policy what should be done in the light of such an assessment. There has to be a division of labour with all the limitations as well as the advantages that this involves.

Finally, there is the all-important issue of the timing of managerial action. It is never enough to decide what to do and how much: it is also necessary to decide *when* to act. It may well be right to do nothing for the time being and to postpone action, recognizing that the need for action may pass or that in due course the right course may be one that is currently inappropriate. It may equally be right to act hastily and without full consideration of the consequences, lest worse befall.

(d) Other limitations on managerial action

Even when the government knows exactly what it wants to do it may be unable to act for purely practical reasons: for example, the limited range of weapons that it can employ or the limited ways in which they can be used. In this country the Government has to rely heavily on persuasion, co-operation and adequate incentives without any assurance as to the degree to which these will be forthcoming. It has no direct control, in the absence of rationing or licensing, over the evolution of consumer demand or over private saving, although it can exercise a powerful indirect influence through the tax system or through varying social service benefits. It has very limited power over the behaviour of wages and prices, especially in the longer run. Its success in meeting foreign competition abroad or even in the home market is necessarily doubtful. Its access to international credit is limited and the willingness of foreigners to go on holding sterling is liable to fluctuate. Investment plans, even when within the public domain, may not work out as expected or intended.

V

So far I have dwelt almost exclusively on aspects of management common to business and government. But the management of the economy is in many ways fundamentally different from the running of a large firm; and I should like to conclude by underlining some of these differences.

One important difference is related to the accountancy of decision-taking. A single business can usually do its sums in money and may have no need to reflect on what lies behind the money-veil. But governments do feel such a need. They have to look beyond the immediate impact of monetary transactions to the ultimate effects on the economy as a whole, including multiplier and accelerator effects and the repercussions on the balance of payments. They have also to think consistently in real terms and ask of alternative money expenditures not merely whether they will bring different benefits or earlier benefits but whether they will make equal claims on real resources. Rules of conduct and systems of accountancy that are the height of wisdom for a private individual or a public company may be the height of folly when practised by governments.

The truth of this has long been recognized in relation to saving and spending. But it is a truth of far wider application since it means adopting a different approach to all forms of government revenue and expenditure from that appropriate to private income and outlay. No government has as yet succeeded in making all the necessary changes in its system of accountancy (although the British Government is as far advanced as any); and every government is bound to be conscious of the confusion and misunderstanding that a dual standard of accountancy must generate in Parliamentary debate and public comment.

This dual standard reflects, secondly, a difference in policy objectives and in the criteria by which policies are judged. The objectives of a single enterprise are different in character from those of a government managing an entire economy, however much both may strive after stability, growth, and an acceptable distribution of income. The individual enterprise usually judges its success in terms of its own prosperity whether or not this marches with the prosperity of the economy while the government is obliged to take a wider view.

This brings us to a third and major difference. One cannot equate the management of the economy with business management because decision-taking by government is always and everywhere a political activity. Decisions are not taken on the basis of some simple calculus of economic gain or loss but have to embrace political considerations as well.

Economic policy does not exist in isolation from other aspects of policy. Although young economists are often taught economics as if one could carve up policy and call this part economic, that part military and that other part cultural, the fact is that policy is a seamless web and that any particular decision must have different elements in it, some of an economic character and some non-economic. The idea, for example, that because devaluation represents operation through an economic variable it should be governed purely by economic considerations is highly naïve. It is equally naïve to think that a Chancellor should frame his Budget without first asking himself whether it would commend itself to the Cabinet, to his Party, or to the House of Commons as currently constituted.

The aims of policy are generally obscure, in conflict, and inconsistent. The weight attached to these aims by different people even within the same party are bound to differ. Some people are inclined to take short views where others are more anxious about the long run. The process by which policy is formed cannot, therefore, be a particularly scientific one or take place with the smoothness so frequently associated in people's minds with the term 'planning'. It must inevitably involve group pressures, heated arguments, intrigues, jockeying for position and all that we associate with politics. This is not because politicians are different from other men, but because the resolution of human conflicts in a peaceful way inevitably involves struggles at the highest level, not only between parties but within them.

It is not possible, therefore, to proceed in the way so often assumed by economists and start from given value judgments already laid down in working out what should be done. *Whose* value judgments? Is it to be supposed that Cabinets never disagree? Or that they never reverse previous decisions, or never yield to pressure, or, for that matter, never give way to other Cabinets? It seems to me a travesty to take for granted that value judgments are more certain and calculable than economic trends.

The fact of political conflict means that what at first sight seem purely technical issues become the subject of party debate. Governments may be inhibited from using particular instruments of policy such as bank rate by ideological considerations or by the force of popular feeling which they have stirred up earlier when in opposition. They may commit themselves publicly to doctrines about how the economy should be run that rest on little more than assertion and then find it impossible to retract when the doctrines are put to the test. Persuasion becomes not merely an act of political leadership but an economic weapon; and skill in managing the economy begins to rest more heavily on proficiency in economic psychiatry than on insight into econometric relationships. One need only look at the gyrations of exchange markets over the past few years to see how political and psychological factors have interacted to complicate the tasks of economic management.

What is new in all this is not the emergence of political and psychological influences in economic affairs—they have always been present—but the pervasiveness of these influences. The expansion of management means simultaneously an increased dependence on government decisions and an increase in the consultations and negotiations preceding these decisions. All this extends the area of psychological warfare. Bluff, rumour, the contrived leak, and other devices come into play. Decisions of policy are influenced more by considerations of prestige, loss of face, announcement effects, immediate negotiability, and so on, and less by ultimate economic advantage. Policy is less flexible and more irreversible.

A democratic government must always be highly dependent on persuasion, most of all when other weapons of policy are inadequate. But this dependence tends to make the government less than frank and assume an air of being in control of events that frequently has little justification. It is not easy for a government to go to the public to ventilate its doubts when everyone expects it to give a lead. This means that there is bound to be some public suspicion of the government and that it is peculiarly difficult to predict in advance how the public will react. The Government may over-play its hand and expose itself to criticisms of cocksureness when in fact it is saturated with private doubts. The uncertainties generated by change itself can easily be multiplied by misunderstandings of this kind.

There is here a difference between the normal situation in government and in business. Government decisions are subject to intense public scrutiny and continuous inquest, or at least the outcomes of decisions are scrutinised and criticised, whereas most business management decisions are secrets unto themselves, mediocre outcomes being more easily attributed to the play of factors outside the scope of the organisation. This makes economic policy decisions, unlike the decentralised mass of business decisions, more subject to misinterpretation and distortion. Indeed, the mass media which have to reach their public by over-simplifying and dramatising economic issues, can generate or magnify uncertainty, and unduly hasten or retard the public expectations of timing and outcomes in a way which is not experienced by business.

VI

What morals can one draw from all this as to the direction that economic analysis should take? If a subject which we may call 'managerial economics' or 'economic administration' is to be developed it will have to blend economic theory and decision theory with realistic analysis of the way in which organisations behave and administrative structures become adapted to the pressures on them. It will need to start from the fact that ignorance is real, prejudice powerful and uncertainty inescapable and consider a wide range of time horizons. For this purpose historical perspective is at least as important as mathematical subtlety. The theory will have to do justice to recorded experience and lend itself to application by busy men impatient of logical refinement (particularly if coupled with footnotes in small print). It will also have to make provision for the weaving together of economic and non-economic considerations: for it is a truth too often ignored that there is no such thing as economic policy in isolation from other aspects of policy—there is only policy.

2

The Economic Planners viewed from inside a large Corporation

F. S. McFadzean*

To plan or not to plan has been a widely debated topic for almost half a century. In Britain support for national planning has come from a wide variety of groups. All political parties have dabbled in it at one time or another. The Trade Unions and the Confederation of British Industry have supported it. Business men have solemnly declared that the perfection of the techniques of national planning is one of the greatest challenges of our time.

The Appeal of National Planning

The planners have considerable emotional appeal. They give the impression that they can accelerate the rate of growth. They have an aura of being purposeful. The feeling that they are controlling events, rather than relying on the unpredictability of the market place, gratifies the will to power in some, the desire for order in others. Support from certain sections of business possibly stems from a mis-placed hope that the stress of having constantly to adjust to an ever changing environment will be reduced if the planners succeed.

The enthusiasm of the planners for their task usually varies in-versely with their knowledge of how the economy operates. The introduction, or reintroduction, of national planning is usually pre-ceded by a generous use of high-sounding and capacious language of little practical content. 'Forging a new Britain in the white heat of the modern technological revolution', 'masters of our destiny', 'ceasing to be victims of blind economic forces', 'taming the jungle', 'impatient to apply the new thinking', 'poised to swing [the] plans into instant operation', and 'restless with positive remedies', are but a few. This is the heady, political froth of the subject; it is only when

* A Managing Director of the Royal Dutch/Shell Group.

the planning process starts that the impossible complexities of the task become more apparent. Statistics for accurate national planning do not exist, stated a frustrated Sir Stafford Cripps in 1946; some two decades later, Mr. George Brown voiced the same complaint in almost identical words.

The substantial limitations of corporate planning will be mentioned later, but all of it—certainly as far as Shell is concerned, and the same is probably true of other corporations—starts off from a given factual position and endeavours to see the way ahead through the vast range of possibilities with a view to taking positive action to achieve the objectives. It is a policy of identifying what we want to do and how we intend to do it. The projections on which the large numbers of investment decisions are made have to be tested and alternatives examined. If projections show substantial deviations from past trends they are probed to ensure that they have a reasonable base and are not the result of wishful thinking. In spite of this, mistakes are still made; but the basic approach is quite different from that adopted by the national planners in 1965. They were not interested in what Shell and other companies intended to do; they set out to ascertain what we would do if certain rates of growth, which nobody could justify and none of us believed, were in some miraculous way to be achieved. We made it clear we had no intention of changing our programme; nevertheless we were required to submit a mass of figures—mainly guesswork since in the time allotted it was impossible to do any accurate estimating—as to what we would do in a completely hypothetical situation.

National Planning without a Mechanism

If all of this had been regarded as an intellectual exercise by the planners then, apart from the not inconsiderable cost involved in collecting and processing the data, no great harm would have been done. However, the aggregation of these largely meaningless statistics—made more meaningless by central adjustments to make the various parts appear more consistent—was published as a plan. What precisely the word 'plan' meant in this context was never quite clear. It certainly did not contain within itself the means of bringing about the results it purported to show. Yet it was occasionally interpreted as something which could, and would, be realised. Unless it were so interpreted there could be no justification for

Mr. Brown's grandiose assertion that 'at last Britain is on its way', or
Mr. Callaghan's claim that the Government had devised 'a new
machine'. Only the interpretation that the compound rate of growth
of 3·8% per annum was going to be achieved could possibly have
justified the rapid increase in Government expenditure. Yet no one
knew, least of all the planners themselves, the mechanism by which
the end result was to be produced.

Sometimes the planners were less definite as to what the 1965 plan
meant. It was occasionally described as a series of signposts high-
lighting some of the problems that had to be solved if a higher rate
of growth were to be achieved. If this were what it really meant a
corrollary should surely have been that no action—such as increased
Government expenditure—which was predicated on the success of
the plan should be taken until the problems were solved and the
increased rate of growth achieved. For the critics who were concerned that the plan was a prelude to a more rapid expansion of an
already over-expanded bureaucracy there was an assurance that it
was indicative only, that the plan would make people expansion-
minded and that this change in approach would in some mysterious
way bring about the expansion. To the sceptic who felt it was a far
cry from collecting statistics as to what people would do in a hypothetical situation to translating the hypothetical situation into
reality, the planners expressed the view that the bridging of the gap
could be achieved by proper use of the Industrial Reconstruction
Corporation, the large battery of Neddies, the Prices and Incomes
Board, the massive purchasing power of the Government and the
nationalized industries, investment grants and the selective employment tax. The precise role, in implementing the plan, of each con-
stituent part of this formidable array of weapons, rests in obscurity.

The Oversimplifications of National Planning

When the 1965 plan was finally discredited all sorts of reasons,
except the real one—that the whole concept of central planning, in
the sense in which it was practised, had no real basis in fact and was
incompatible with the existence of an economy which was subject to
both national and international market forces over a large range of
its production and consumption—were adduced for its failure.
Mr. Catherwood assured us that it would be replaced by 'realistic'
planning—a euphemism which merely highlighted the fact that the

planners themselves were in disagreement. The first sentence of *The Task Ahead, Economic Assessment to* 1972 assures us that it is 'a planning document and not a plan', whatever that phrase is intended to imply about the validity and influence on policy of the statistics set forth in the document. Abandoning the whole concept as a failure was unthinkable. After mentioning the long lead in time in the construction of refineries and chemical plants, Mr. Catherwood sought to justify the continuation of central planning on the grounds that 'Technology brings greater capital intensity and the cost of faulty decisions—to the companies, to the economy as a whole—rises'. That advanced technology brings greater capital intensity is a well known fact; the proposition that the cost of faulty decisions rises is also correct in an absolute sense but more doubtful in a relative sense. It depends on the scale of the business and the rate of growth. Thus, if between the two world wars Shell had produced, through faulty decisions—which incidentally are only recognised after, not before, the event—a surplus of 1m. tons of ships the effect on our business would have been considerable. To-day a surplus of 1m. tons would be overtaken by demand in a few months. Moreover, the loss of interest on the money involved—the main cost of investing prematurely—would be largely offset by cost inflation. Mr. Catherwood's assertion therefore requires some qualification; however, it does crystallise several of the defects of the planners—their over-simplification of complex issues, their assumption of superior wisdom denied to lesser mortals making investment decisions in the various companies and their failure to grasp the logical outcome of the policies they are advocating.

Many years ago Professor Jewkes highlighted the tendency of the planners to overlook the wide variety of products in the industrial system and to view problems 'in the round'. The planners are inclined to talk of items like thread and textiles as if they are homogeneous commodities. As Professor Jewkes pointed out 'there are several thousand kinds of sewing thread and hundreds of different kinds of textile products, each produced to meet a separate need'. Refineries and chemical plants are not standardised entities. Few of the many Shell refineries world-wide are identical in size—none of them are identical in capital cost, running cost or the range of end products which they manufacture. Discussions about investing in a chemical plant (or even a petrochemical plant) have about as much practical relevance as talking about investing in propulsion without specifying whether it is air, marine or land, internal or external combustion, large or small horsepower. Shell and other companies produce hundreds of different chemicals. The capital cost of the plants involved varies widely. Each chemical is aimed at a specific market with its own characteristics and subjected to its own particular competitive pressures.

Consensus a Mirage

In view of the record in this country, the assumption that the intervention of the amateur planner is going to eliminate or reduce costly investment errors by the private sector is an interesting one. Apparently the planners are of the view that if each company disclosed its investment programme and we all entered into dialogues a 'consensus' would emerge which would prevent over- or under-investment in particular lines of capital equipment. It is naïve of the planners to think that companies will disclose these figures and discuss them with their competitors. Investment programmes inevitably reflect the marketing strategy and judgments of all the companies concerned. In many instances—and these are likely to increase as business becomes more international—investments in the United Kingdom are affected by a company's strategy in other countries. So the planners, if they are to make any sense out of the figures at all, will have to demand an ever widening range of information. The companies in turn will only be able to make sense out of the planners if they have access to all the data which justified whatever decisions are reached. This would involve each company having knowledge of the plans of all other companies. In a competitive environment this is absurd so it would probably finish up by the planners handing down their edicts without anyone, apart from the planners, being able to understand how the decisions were reached.

Moreover, assuming a 'consensus' were achieved on, for example, such an elementary point as the estimated total demand for varying oil products in the United Kingdom in 1975, there is no *prima facie* reason to believe that the consensus figures will be more accurate in practice than the estimates of the individual companies. These are bound to vary from company to company, and the differences will, in part at least, cancel each other out. Where estimating is done on a monolithic basis the errors—and errors there must inevitably be— are liable to be monolithic also. This has been particularly true in the past of investment decisions in the centralised coal and electricity industries in the United Kingdom.

There is no evidence to justify Mr. Catherwood's basic contention that central planning will eliminate or reduce such errors as are from time to time made by individual companies planning their own investment programmes in various refineries, different chemical plants or any other capital equipment. Moreover the logical conclusion of his claim for the efficacy of central planning is that a predetermined market will, by means of licensing, or in some other fashion which prevents companies from implementing their own plans, be shared out among the companies concerned. If newcomers are excluded the established companies will sit comfortably on their market shares. If newcomers are permitted to compete the need not to exceed the overall targets will require a scaling down in the plans of the existing companies. We are back once more in the era of the bureaucrat determining who will move over; and the newcomer will thereby be permitted to establish himself much more easily than he would under a system of free enterprise. Moreover the scope for companies to change their plans would have to be restricted, since failure to implement any particular share could result in the market going short. This must be the end result of Mr. Catherwood's approach to planning if the words he uses have any meaning at all. 'Co-operation' and striving to reach a consensus in any industry which is competitive must largely destroy the competition.

Industrial critics of 'national planning' are often accused of inconsistency; as the *Financial Times* put it in a leading article: 'Any big company these days after all has to plan on the basis of a medium —or even long term—assessment of future trends. There is no reason why the country as a whole should not benefit from a similar approach, as long as it is understood by all concerned that what is being produced is a series of forecasts subject to revision and not targets which will or must be achieved.' Further refined, this view is a compound of three interrelated ideas. There is firstly the notion that the purpose of planning—whether 'national' or corporate—is to reduce the area of uncertainty. On this view the merit of a plan must vary inversely with the area of its residual uncertainty. Secondly it is supposed that the corporate planners know how to do this kind of planning successfully. Thirdly it is assumed that despite the truly massive differences in scale and complexity the parallels between the kind of operation the corporate planners are believed to engage in and the kind of exercise the national planners want to undertake are so many and so strong that the latter may safely follow the same trail as the corporate planner. These views are, to a considerable extent, dangerous and misleading; since they seem to be close to the heart of the controversy they will form the core of this paper.

Galbraith on Corporate Planning

A great deal of confusion has been caused by the pronouncements of certain economists on the role of the corporate planner. The most articulate of these, and the one that probably commands the greatest following, is Professor Galbraith. Most of you are no doubt familiar with his views but let me try to summarize the relevant part very briefly. He divides corporations neatly into two groups—entrepreneurial corporations and mature corporations. In the former, management and share ownership are substantially in the same hands; in the latter they are effectively divorced. Although he does not define precisely what he means by maximum profit, Professor Galbraith accepts that this is the motivating factor in the entre-preneurial corporation. In the mature corporation, however, power is effectively vested in the technostructure—the conglomerate of managers, engineers, chemists, accountants and so forth, without which the operation and planning of a modern business would not be possible—and there is no *a priori* reason why this group of people should toil to maximize profits for a largely faceless and unknown group of shareholders. Their motivation, says Professor Galbraith, is survival and to survive they must preserve their autonomy. This objective is achieved not by maximising profit, which can be hazardous, but by earning a level sufficient to pay a dividend that will keep the shareholders from interfering in the business and enable sufficient money to be ploughed back to make the technostructure independent of the capital market. Subsidiary to the main motivation is the greatest possible rate of corporate growth as measured in sales.

The mature corporation achieves its objectives of profitability and reducing uncertainty to the minimum by planning; but planning and the market economy are incompatible bedfellows. A substitute for the latter is necessary and several are possible. Vertical integration from the raw material to the final consumer eliminates the market at each successive functional stage of a business. Short of complete integration the mature corporation can use the pressure of its massive buying power to dictate the prices charged by its suppliers. The planners not only control backwards; they control forwards and by advertising and other means manipulate the consumers to take the quantity of goods they produce at the prices the planners dictate. Such is the ability of the corporate planners to insulate themselves from market forces and achieve a pre-determined level of profit that in certain cases the power they exercise makes them 'conceivably omnipotent'.

Professor Galbraith's assertions as to how the planning process is conducted in a mature corporation bears no relationship to any reality that we have experienced in Shell. Far from feeling 'conceivably omnipotent' the predominant hope is that the multiplicity of judgments being exercised on a continuous basis at many levels in the Group, and in the many countries in which we function, will prove on balance to be more right than wrong. Elimination of uncertainty, says Professor Galbraith, is the main goal of the planner; we have learned to live with the fact that the planner who can eliminate uncertainty does not exist.

The Sources of Uncertainty

Uncertainties stem from many sources. There is first of all the vast range of uncertainties that are political in their origin and which can have far reaching effects on our business. Sometimes these are sensed as possibilities; in many cases it cannot be predicted with any certainty that they will occur at all or, if they do, precisely when. Which planner forecast, any time ahead, the date of the Arab-Israeli war and the closure of the Suez Canal and who forecast that it would remain closed for as long as it has? Who can forecast to-day when it will reopen? Who forecast five years, or even one year, before the event that sterling would devalue in November 1967? Who five years ago forecast the tragedy of the Nigerian civil war? These and many other political events have had major effects on our business, yet none of us forecast them with any degree of accuracy.

There is the uncertainty which arises as a result of technological progress. The speed of change, and the long lead in time between designing a plant and its coming on stream, make it almost inevitable that the plant will, to some extent, be obsolete in the light of developments effected since it was designed. This requires a sense of balance and judgment. Even in the process of designing modern sophisticated equipment more efficient ways are found to do a specific task. This in turn can necessitate the redesigning of other parts of the plant. It is a continuous process and somewhere along the line designs have to be frozen otherwise the project would never leave the drawing board. Sometimes new developments can be grafted on to an already existing plant; in other cases this proves impossible. Thus many of the tankers in the 40,000/50,000 ton class which at the time of their launching were hailed, and rightly so, as great steps forward, will have to be scrapped before the end of their physical lives since they will not be able to compete with the 200,000 tonners coming into service in large numbers. The 200,000 tonners were made possible by many factors. There were improvements in shipbuilding techniques; there were improvements in engine design which enabled these ships to be driven by a single screw; there were improvements in loading and discharging facilities at the various ports; there was the improvement in techniques for lightening the large ships at sea and a host of other, often in themselves minor, developments which made these vessels the attractive economic proposition they are to-day. These ships have at least a twenty-year life. The question is whether they in turn will become obsolete in the light of future developments. Nobody really knows with any degree of certainty. We would guess that well within the next ten years a tanker of one million tons will be technically feasible. Whether such a ship will be economic however depends on numerous factors, many of which are still unknowns. It would be a bold planner indeed who would eliminate this uncertainty by giving a categorical answer one way or the other.

There is the uncertainty which arises from physical factors outside the planners' control. For example, a severe winter in Europe or the Eastern Seaboard of the United States of America can have quite a dramatic effect on the demand for various oil products. It affects volumes, it affects prices and affects the freight rates for tankers. On the basis of historical records we can make guesses on temperatures; we are never able to prognosticate them in any given year with accuracy. There is also the physical uncertainty involved in the search for crude oil and natural gas—the basic raw materials of the industry. Considerable advances have been made over the years in exploration techniques but no one has yet devised a means for determining the location of hydrocarbons without drilling. Seismic and other geophysical techniques can indicate where there are possibilities of accumulations; only by drilling can their existence be proved or disproved. Although the odds vary from area to area the overall odds against drilling and finding any oil or gas are nine to one. The overall odds against drilling and finding oil or gas in commercial quantities are thirty to one. Many millions of pounds can be spent in exploration and the results can vary throughout a range from zero to accumulations so large as to have an appreciable effect on world markets and other producing areas. The possibilities open to the planners for eliminating this uncertainty are minimal. It is a fact of life with which we have learned to live, although we, and others, engage in constant research to improve the techniques of exploration.

There is the uncertainty of the market place. Professor Galbraith's assertion that a large corporation can insulate itself from the market, by integrating backwards on the one hand and reaching forward to bend the consumer to take what is produced at a pre-determined price on the other, is so startling in its implications that he ought to have produced a great deal of evidence to support it. Professor Galbraith relies a lot on the automobile industry to justify his arguments; I have shown elsewhere that his assertions are not supported by the experience of the American or British motor car industries. Nor are they true of oil. None of the large international companies is fully integrated in the sense that Professor Galbraith uses the phrase but even if they were, they would only suppress the market as far as they were concerned and not their competitors. Whether integration will produce an advantage or not depends on many factors, of which the most important is probably the cost of achieving it. Thus after the first Suez crisis in 1956 Shell ordered a lot of tankers and undertook an extensive long-term chartering programme. Due to the overloading of shipyards the costs of doing this were high. Subsequently ship-building capacity expanded rapidly and the cost of new buildings fell. At the same time the advances in ship design culminating in the 200,000 tonners and above rendered a lot of the vessels we had ordered and chartered uneconomic long before the end of their physical lives. Companies which had not integrated backwards and newcomers to the industry found themselves at a cost advantage over Shell. When I read of the great power supposedly wielded by the corporate planners I cannot help pondering that if any person, whether a planner or not, could forecast accurately over the next twelve months (let alone five years ahead) the tanker rates prevailing in the Persian Gulf for single voyage, consecutive voyage and twelve month charters, he would literally be able to earn millions of pounds; and this is only a small part of our business. In practice it is a continuous exercise of judgment in the face of many unknown factors. It is quite impossible to ensure that the judgment will be correct but it is the skill with which it is exercised that can in substantial measure determine the success of a company.

What has been said about tankers is true of the whole range of our business. It is open to us to explore for and produce our own crude oil or buy from or sell to others; we can use our own ships, charter in or charter out on a single voyage, consecutive voyage or long-term arrangement; we can build our own refineries, process crude oil for other companies or process crude oil in other refineries; we can buy refined products in bulk or we can sell them in bulk; we can distribute through jobbers or direct to consumers; we can sell or buy spot or forward over long periods; we can use our own road tankers for distribution or contract out to specialist road haulage firms. We do all of these things to a varying degree, in different places and at different times. The criterion is which in our judgment is likely to produce the maximum profitability. At each stage there is a market. Although, as already mentioned, the corporate planner may try to suppress it as far as his own company is concerned, he cannot do it for his competitors. It would be a foolhardy man indeed who would plan to have his corporation fully integrated over a period of years. Judgments are too fallible and the unexpected happens too often to justify such an approach.

Professor Galbraith's statement that the corporate planners can reach forward and bend the consumer to take the quantity produced at a pre-determined price seems to me quite incredible. It is not true of the automobile industry; it is not true of the oil industry. Professor Allen and others have given several other examples to disprove Professor Galbraith's contention. Let me add one more. In the first six months of this year oil prices in Japan have fallen sharply. Profits, where they are being earned, are minimal; some companies are making a loss. Not only did the corporate planners not plan this change; most of them did not even foresee it was going to happen a few months, let alone a few years, before it did.

The Aim of Corporate Planning

Having brought the corporate planner down from the Olympian heights to which he ought not to have been elevated by Professor

Galbraith, what is the objective of corporate planning? It can be argued that the reduction of uncertainty is one of the aims but the residual area of uncertainty is so large that if this were the standard by which planning were to be judged we, in Shell at least, would regard it as a failure. The objective is much more modest; it is to produce a flow of information and ideas on the alternative allocation of resources open to us. It is not only a question of the capital and manpower necessary to meet our anticipated share of expanding markets; we are equally concerned with the use being made of existing resources and how what we are already doing can be performed more efficiently.

Planning, in the way in which Shell conducts it, is a continuing process. At the beginning of every year we review our estimates for six years ahead; the estimates are updated approximately eight months later in the light of major developments which have taken place in the interim. No investment decisions are made at the planning meetings. General lines of policy are laid down and the literally hundreds of projects that result are progressively developed and justified separately on the basis, where appropriate, of earning power and pay-out time.

Decentralised Forward Assessments

The collection of the data necessary for the broad decisions of policy is fairly decentralised. Within a general statistical framework, the manager in each of the many countries in which Shell operates makes his own forward assessments. The demand for energy is derived from the demand for other things which are largely functions of an economy's overall development—transport, iron and steel production, machinery, domestic heating, and so forth. While there are exceptions, most assessments of future growth in gross domestic product are based on a continuation of the historical trend. The translation of the trend in gross domestic product into the trend in the demand for energy is again usually made on the basis of historic ratios. In the United Kingdom the ratio (energy/gross domestic product) is 0·62: 1; the corresponding figures are 0·64 in Western Germany, 0·76 in the U.S.A. and 0·87 in France. The ratios are of course determined by many factors. For example, in the United Kingdom nearly one-third of the primary energy consumed is used as fuel in power stations. Because of the tonnages involved, improvements in the efficiency of conversion can have a significant bearing on the demand for primary energy. An improvement of 1% for example would produce a saving of 1 million tons of coal equivalent per annum. Since the early 1950s the average efficiency of power stations has improved from 23% to 27/28%, a rate of improvement of 1·4% per annum over the period as a whole. Whether this rate will continue or accelerate—there are stations that operate at 35% plus efficiency— is difficult to say with any assurance. Again, American experience would indicate that faster growth itself will move the ratio up. Nevertheless, and although the results may not be completely accurate, the various ratios have hitherto been sufficiently stable to justify their continued use. **1560244**

Having obtained a view of the probable demand trend for energy as a whole, it is is necessary to assess the part likely to be played in the total picture by coal, oil, natural gas and atomic power. This involves not only weighing up the relative economic strength of the various forms of primary energy in the demand areas in which they are competitive; it involves also an assessment of the policies of various governments such as, for example, the protection of coal by a tax on fuel oil in the United Kingdom, or possible anti-pollution measures in Japan which could result in fuel oil being displaced for certain uses by imports of liquefied natural gas. A profile is finally built up of the role likely to be played by the various oil products in the total picture and the share of that total which, in the light of the competitive picture in each country, Shell hopes to obtain. The individual country plans are brought together and aggregated with estimates of bunkers, aviation products, crude oil and other central sales. The totals are then translated into approximate capital requirements to produce the necessary crude oil, tankers, refining and marketing assets involved. The many alternative ways of meeting the anticipated market demand are examined and consideration is also given to the possible repercussions if some of the basic assumptions and prognostications are not realised in practice.

All the component parts of a plan compiled in this way are suspect to varying degrees. The time taken to collect and process the data makes it to some extent out-of-date before the final document is produced. Most suspect of all are the forward projections of the trend of prices of the various oil products in each country. Here we have seldom been right so that earning powers and pay-out times, calculated on such estimates, are viewed with a great deal of scepticism.

Although our costs are affected by factors outside our control—selective employment tax and inflation for example—it is our cost trends that we can probably influence more than any other aspect of our business. Contrary to Professor Galbraith's assertions, we know that our detailed profit forecasts are likely to be wrong; but if we can improve our costs relative to our competitors we should, over a period at least, be able to put up a satisfactory profit performance. Most generalisations are suspect and there are many reasons for corporate planning. Trying to estimate what the consumer wants and producing it at the lowest possible cost are by far the most important.

Let the rate of growth look after itself

The aspirations of the national planners are quite different from the corporate planners'. Their *raison d'être* lies in the validity of their claims to be able to accelerate the rate of growth beyond what it would be without their intervention. This is a claim which, by its very nature, can never be completely proved or disproved since nobody can know for certain what developments would have been if the planners had not existed. Yet, from a purely practical viewpoint, their claims involve them at the outset in a major dilemma. Irrespective of the rate of growth prevailing at the time they intervene, their plans cannot envisage a slower rate—the politicians would not stand for it. They cannot envisage the continuation of the historical trend; this would raise the question of why the planners were necessary since the trend had hitherto been achieved without their intervention. So the planners have to plan a rate of growth higher than the historical trend but there is no scientific or rational basis for determining what the higher rate should be. There have been many learned books and discussions on the factors which cause economic growth and many explanations to account for the high rates in Japan and Germany and the low rate in the United Kingdom. However, the idea that any economist, or group of economists (or politicians for that matter), can plan a particular rate of growth and the means of achieving it is a pretentious one which is unsupported by any valid evidence. At best an atmosphere conducive to growth can be created; the rate of growth should be left to look after itself. Increases, or decreases, in government expenditure should be determined by a factual analysis of the current position, not by wishful thinking about a future expansion in gross domestic product which exists only in the imagination of the planners.

I hope I have said enough to disprove Professor Galbraith's theories about the powers vested in corporate planners and to show that the argument, that national planning is merely corporate planning writ large, is largely baseless. It is doubtful if the national planners really believe the latter. I suspect the argument is simply a rationalisation to excuse past failures, to justify their continued existence and to condone their persistent indulgence in intervention. Mr. Attlee once remarked to Professor Laski that a prolonged period of silence would be the most useful contribution he could make; the planners might also take this piece of socialist advice to heart.

3

Management and Control in Eastern European Economies

Prof. Alec Nove*

What is management?

The subject is a vast one. 'Eastern Europe' consists of many states, of different size, historical tradition, resource endowment and managerial forms. In this whole area—broadly defined here as including all communist-ruled countries in Europe—the planning system was at one time identical with the Russian, since the Soviet model was copied in matters great and small. This is certainly no longer the case. Consequently an adequate survey of the arrangements of each country would occupy an impossible amount of space. We in Glasgow have just begun to undertake a comparative study of reform of industrial planning and management, with the help of a grant made available by SSRC. The work will take two years and will result in six country studies and a general volume.

In all these circumstances it is easy to understand why the field has to be covered selectively. Two countries will receive special attention: the Soviet Union and Hungary. They represent respectively the 'conservative' and 'radical' approach to reform of the system inherited from the Stalin area.

It is also desirable to be clear from the first as to what is meant by 'management' and 'control'. These apparently simple terms, if applied to a Soviet-type economy, can cause great confusion of thought. Too easily is it assumed that an enterprise director is a 'manager', and the ministry, Gosplan, the government, are controllers, who make plans which the manager carries out. But of course this will not do at all. The 'enterprise' is normally synonymous

* Bonar Professor of Economics and Director of the Institute of Soviet and East European Studies of the University of Glasgow.

with a plant or factory. In manufacturing (this paper will be concerned primarily with manufacturing industry), the Soviet director is thus a plant manager. The proper analogy in the west is the plant manager within the corporation. The 'traditional' Soviet equivalent of the *corporation* management is to be found at ministerial level, either in the ministry itself (I.C.I. or Du Pont equals the Ministry of Chemical Industry) or one of its administrative sub-divisions, the so-called 'chief departments' (*glavki*). So the industrial ministry is seen as an integral part of the management structure, though it is also a means of control on behalf of superior authority. But then one must ask: who or what *is* superior authority? Suppose one envisages the entire Soviet (or Polish, or Rumanian) industry as a single firm. Then those in charge of U.S.S.R. Ltd. are its top *management*.

These points are made not because of any perverse desire for paradoxes, but because they really are germane to an understanding both of the nature of the traditional centralised system and of the problems posed by trying to reform it. It is therefore worth dwelling upon these matters a little while longer.

One must, for example, deal with an objection to the above approach. Surely, it will be said, there is such a thing as political control over the economy, or politically-motivated interference with economic processes, or non-economic choices, reflected in 'planners' preferences'. These political decisions are imposed upon the management by ministers and through ministries. They reflect and express the politically-determined priorities of the regime.

This objection is to considerable degree valid, and so the picture requires to be modified to accommodate it. Thus the very top 'management' of the great firm U.S.S.R. Ltd is the politbureau of the ruling party, and plainly it has aims and responsibilities which are not, in the usual sense of that term, 'managerial'; certainly not solely managerial. Nevertheless, among their principal preoccupations is that of running the economy. They may decide strategic questions, but also smaller ones too: the need to expand fuel output, and within it oil and gas; or develop electronics; or encourage the expansion of canning facilities in rural areas; or increase the relative importance of profits in computing managerial bonuses; or decide to increase minimum wages; or to settle an argument about the location of a particular factory. Sometimes the politbureau would intervene to ensure that some particular project dear to its collective heart got extra supplies of ball-bearings. The politbureau might also decide to send a rude note to China, expand the deployment of ICBMs, order the arrest of a dissident writer.

Of course, no one doubts that some politbureau or governmental business is not concerned with the economy. More difficult to classify is the business that is unquestionably economic, but where there is an element, which *may* be dominant, that could be called 'political'. I cannot pretend that I have discovered any clear dividing line. Perhaps it is best simply to point out, by way of examples, the sort of problems involved here.

We can all think of basic policy decisions about the economy— and not only in the U.S.S.R.—which are undoubtedly politically inspired. However, the line to be drawn between 'political' and economic *policy* is not by any means a clear one. Then it is also the case that many decisions are derived, are consequences of other decisions and of circumstances. These could be input-output-type consequences: as when steel needs iron ore, houses need furniture, or peasants need incentives if they are to produce the needed crops. In the process of deciding how broadly-defined politically-deter- mined objectives are to be fulfilled, choices are made. The men who make the choices could be politbureau members or ministers. Their motives, like those of men anywhere, may be mixed. However, many are beyond doubt managerial, and do not cease to be such merely because they are not taken by reference to the market. A minister of chemical industry may order 'his' enterprises to produce more sulphuric acid because, either in his opinion, or in that of the central planners, more sulphuric acid will be needed in 1971. We cannot seriously assert that this is a 'political' decision, whereas the manag- ing director of I.C.I., issuing a perhaps identical instruction to *his* subordinates, is acting as a super-manager.

One source of analytical confusion is a misrepresentation of the nature of conflicts between different levels of the Soviet-managerial system. These conflicts are sometimes seen as one between political and managerial levels, and sometimes this is indeed so. But often the conflicts arise out of differences of motivation and contradictions between incentives.

Let us take one example. Suppose that a ministry issues instruc- tions to increase the output of frankfurters, and rejects the enterprise proposal to produce more salami. (Something very like this did happen.) This cannot be ascribed to a political (or 'planners') preference for the one rather than the other. Why should the minister or Gosplan or Kosygin care about sausage? The following could be the underlying reasons for the conflict:

(a) The Food industry ministry is under pressure from the Internal Trade ministry, which reflects complaints about non-availability of frankfurters.

(b) The enterprise is seeking to fulfil an output plan in tons. Salami is heavier.

(c) The Food industry ministry may have a plan in roubles; frankfurters may fit this plan better than salami.

(d) The enterprise may be particularly interested in a bonus based on lowering of unit costs, or in a labour-productivity plan, for which purposes the production of salami happens to be more advantageous.

(e) The local retail trade outlets refuse to buy frankfurters because they are oversupplied, and require more salami, a fact ignored by the ministerial planners.

It will be observed that in case (a) the ministry is reflecting consumer demand, in the case of (e) it is the enterprise, in the other instances the various plan indicators seem to have no connection with demand for different types of sausage and managerial behaviour consists of adaptation to aggregated plans.

In other words—and this is a point to appreciate if one is to understand one essential argument for reform—no one actually preferred any assortment of sausage, or indeed any other product—except, of course, the consumer. To cite a Soviet writer, who discusses the same point using another example: 'the state does not need cups and plates, the citizen needs crockery'.[1] If salami and frankfurters, cups and plates, television sets and radios, wool cloth and mixtures, are produced in proportions which differ from consumer demand, this is usually an undesired consequence of the operation of the system, not the result of conscious aims. Incentives, indicators, prices, cause distortions.

'Centralised pluralism'

Distortions of another kind arise out of the nature of the 'central planners'. One can conceive of the entire planning-managerial

---

[1] P. Volin. *Novyi mir*, No. 3, 1969, p. 56. (The author put these words into the mouth of a Hungarian planner.)

apparatus as one vast hierarchy, and indeed this is the juridical position (except for the complication of the special role of the Communist party organs, which we will leave aside for the moment). None
the less, it is perhaps equally useful to regard the 'centre' as a set of
autonomous units competing with one another. They all 'belong' to
the state, but so do BEA and British Rail, so it is clear that joint
ownership does not eliminate the competitive element. Even in universities, is is not unknown for different departments or schools to
compete for scarce funds. In the Soviet case, no one can doubt that
each ministry represents an interest, pressing its own claims on
resources and seeking to influence plans for its own advantage. This
affects resource allocation. Soviet critics have pointed out that a
decision to produce more of x, or invest in y rather than z, might
depend on the influence wielded by the minister, or the skill with
which the case is put forward. (Of course, such things are not unknown within western corporations!)

Indeed, enterprise management too makes proposals, and these,
as will be shown, are an essential part of the information-gathering
process without which planning would be impossible. An eminent
Hungarian economist went so far as to remark, in conversation with
me: 'the use of the term "command economy" to describe the
centralised planning system is misleading: more often than not, the
recipients of the commands have themselves written them'.

The centralisation of the 'traditional' Soviet-type economy requires to be carefully qualified. Indeed, our use of the very term
'centralisation' is really rather loose. Juridically all is simple: in a
hierarchy, A is a subordinate of B. But suppose that B cannot act
unless on information supplied by A. Or A's proposals, though sometimes modified by B, usually serve as the basis of what A does. Or the
orders of B to A are aggregated ('x roubles' worth of footwear, or y
tons of metal goods'), so that the subordinate in fact decides the
product mix. Any unambiguous order by B to A must be obeyed, let
us say, but in practice B has neither the time nor the knowledge to
issue orders save in a small proportion of cases. The point of all these
quite realistic examples is that, if one wishes to forecast the effect of
measures which change incentives or motivation at enterprise-
managerial level, it is necessary to take into account the *real* (not the
juridical) extent to which decisions are either taken or influenced by
managers.

Let us now look briefly, in the light of the foregoing, at the principles underlying the traditional planning system. These are:

(1) Resource allocation is by administrative decisions, not through the market.

(2) These decisions to be based on assessment of social needs, reflecting, as regards the volume and direction of investment, the time and other preference of the planners.

(3) The needs so assessed are a combination of the requirements of the state as such (guns, schools, collected works of Lenin) and of the estimates made about consumer requirements (based on demand, modified in some instances by the state's own social preferences, e.g. for less vodka and more vitamins).

(4) Since needs exceed the means of satisfying them, the priority of particular sectors becomes a matter of planners' or political decision.

(5) Enterprises, retailers, farms and other users of goods *indent* for them, by submitting applications (*zayavki*). These must be turned into production and supply plans by various administrative organs. Rules determine who can decide what. Thus some key materials are allocated between principal users by the Council of Ministers of the U.S.S.R., others by Gosplan, or Gossnab (the State Supplies Committees), or by republican organs, or by industrial ministries. Some investment decisions are individually taken on the highest level, others are subject merely to overall 'limits' (*x* roubles for the Food industry), still others are decentralised to enterprise management.

All in all, the plan is based upon a mass of detailed applications, reports, returns, central policy guidance. Experts in Gosplan must concoct a consistent long-term plan, with which major investment decisions are closely related. They must also—and *this* is the labour-intensive part of the process—issue the vast multitude of current orders (instructions) down the hierarchy of ministries, republics, departments, enterprises, supply-offices and the like, so that in the end all enterprises are given plans to fulfil. These must specify output, product mix, customers, suppliers, financial targets, labour and wages plans and so on. It is this operational plan which must be disaggregated into millions of detailed instructions. The subordinate units are judged by whether they fulfil them. Indeed obedience to orders is their one operational criterion in the 'traditional' system. Conscious assessment of need by the party and state machine *replaces* the market. Prices play no active role, and, in so far as resource allocation is concerned, turn into an accounting and auditing device.

For reasons no doubt familiar to many, this apparently highly centralised system suffers from strain. Stalin once made the far-reaching claim that it made possible the substitution of the general for the partial interest: the advantage of the whole took precedence over private short-term profit. However:

(1) The sheer scale of the task requires its division. Hence the multiple levels of the hierarchy, and many units at each level. Hence 'centralised pluralism', already referred to.

(2) The separate units and levels have to deal with related matters, creating acute problems of co-ordination at the centre, and inconsistency of plans at local levels (e.g. as between inputs and output, i.e. production and supply plans, and between both and financial plans, and so on).

(3) The interest of each unit of the hierarchy is primary for its own managers. They are as likely as any capitalist firm to neglect what for it are externalities. Hence examples of 'departmentalism', 'regionalism' and similar deviations. Gosplan and other governmental and party co-ordinating agencies can only combat particularism in a few priority cases, and have neither the time nor the information to do so in the large majority of instances. In any case, they too are divided within themselves into sectional departments with interests of their own.

(4) Pluralist particularism can take the form, already noted, of competition for resources, especially investment funds. It also greatly affects what actually happens at micro level because of the problems, familiar to 'Sovietologists', of success indicators. This problem arises because, in the absence of time and sufficient information, plans have to be made in *aggregated* form: so many tons, roubles, or square metres, or per cent increase in productivity, or reduction in costs. The tendency then is to make whatever fits this measure, and this distorts the product mix and imposes losses on the user, be he another enterprise or a citizen.

(5) The system contains no built-in spur to enterprise or innovation in lower managerial echelons. It is easier to fulfil an easy plan. Risk-taking is not rewarded. Central organs find it necessary to combat inertia, but lack the micro-information required to do so effectively.

There are sometimes orders given of the type: 'introduce 318 innovations during the year', which can stimulate wasteful activities.

(6) Prices based at best on cost-plus fail to convey information as to what is wanted, or the best means to achieve a given end. Neither relative scarcity nor demand changes are conveyed by such prices. Therefore, while an input-output *consistency* is possible (at least at the aggregated level at which material balances are drawn up by planners), the economically most effective way is often unperceived. Input-output tables are of their nature technologically 'conservative', being based on past experience.

(7) The situation has been persistently complicated by the phenomenon of *excess demand*. Consumers' goods tend to be underpriced, *planned* demand for investment goods usually exceeds supply, i.e. the plan is not balanced. One reason for this is that *aggregated* balance is consistent with micro-imbalance (e.g. total planned value of tractor spares may equal total demand, but within it there are excess pistons and too few carburettors). Since the plans envisage full utilization of resources, there is little flexibility. Fear of supply breakdown leads to hoarding at all levels. Each enterprise, each ministry, seeks to make its own components, procure various supplies, duplicating similar activities and disrupting attempts to achieve specialised production and supply arrangements. One of the principal functions of the central planning organs is in fact to ration producers' goods between users, by the system of material allocation.

Efficiency for what?

Is the system then 'inefficient'? To answer this question adequately is no easy matter. It is not enough to point to micro-inefficiencies. Any centralised economies, including the western war economies in (say) 1943, are in one sense inefficient. But plainly this does not entitle us to assert that the war economy should have been based on a decentralised free market, even if it could be shown that the bureaucratic micro-irrationalities would have disappeared. For the purpose of waging war, the *system* of central control was in fact efficient. No alternative system was tolerable or was tolerated. It is a fairly widespread view, on which I will not dwell, that the 'Stalin' economic system was designed to concentrate resources on priority sectors by war-economy methods. Our picture of the logic of growth strategy is perhaps rather too blurred, or too controversial,[1] to enable us to define micro-efficiency with confidence. The same is true of investment criteria. Any system is capable of achieving waste through error, and it is at least arguable that error due to uncertainty is somewhat less likely in a centrally planned economy.

But after allowing for all these factors, it remains the case that the inefficiency of the 'traditional' system is widely argued in the U.S.S.R. itself, and reform is at least on the agenda. This is no place to analyse all the reasons for this. Suffice it to emphasise the importance of one factor: a modified view of the object of economic activity. While still insisting on the priority of the state's own needs, especially in weapons and the means of making them, the Soviet leadership lay stress also on consumers' goods, housing, agriculture, services. It is not enough simply to plan growth, enforce a high level of savings/ investment, direct resources centrally to a few key sectors. Growth continues, but now considerations of quality, the patterns of demand, choices between alternative means and ends, require much greater consideration. The greater the stress on multiplicity of ends, the greater the complexity of centralised planning (which requires a con-centration on a few well-defined priority objectives, such as a war or the creation of heavy industry), the greater also the consciousness of relative scarcity in relation to the many competing ends. The term 'efficiency' gradually comes to take on a meaning familiar to western economists. 'Rationality' becomes no longer primarily develop-mental, though growth remains a major objective of policy, but increasingly a matter of economic use of existing resources. Invest-ment choices, which were discussed in Soviet literature under Stalin in terms of alternative ways of producing more of some particular commodity, now raise problems about comparing *different* products and different ways of making them. The 'economic optimum' begins to be discussed. The 'simultaneous equations', dear to early critics of socialism, are discussed too. The great Russian mathematical tradi-tion, the pioneering work of Kantorovich on linear programming, plus the technical advances in electronic computation, facilitate— after some delay due to dogmatic ideological resistance—the emer-gence of a powerful mathematical-economics school.

---

[1] If Hirschman, Myrdal, Little, Friedman and Bauer were asked to define rational resource allocation in a developing economy, it is unlikely that their report would be unanimous.

All the above can readily be documented by reference to Soviet books and articles in the period 1956–69. Of course more strictly political factors were also relevant: original thought was hardly possible in the 'Stalin' intellectual climate, and so some of the new ideas had to await his death.

New ideas on planning and management

Naturally the new ideas led to a reassessment of the structure of management. The deficiencies listed in the preceding pages were thoroughly aired, and large numbers of proposals for change were put forward. Some envisaged the maintenance of the centralised structure of control more or less intact, with perhaps a little more freedom of choice for lower management levels in deciding the detailed product mix by agreement with the customers. Others went much further, in effect arguing for a socialist market. Prices would fluctuate, managers at 'enterprise' (i.e. plant) level would seek to maximise profits, and the role of the central planners would be confined to taking strategic investment decisions, exercising fiscal (not physical) controls and laying down the rules of the socialist-market game. This (plus election of management by the employees) is the Yugoslav model. Something very like it is implied by the ideas of Ota Šik[1], and, as we shall see, also by the Hungarian reform. The Soviet 'marketeers' are best represented by the publicist G. Lisichkin[2], and not, as is widely believed, by Liberman. The latter does indeed advocate the use of profits as the indicator of enterprise performance. However, he nowhere expressed any explicit view in favour of a socialist *market*, or about the role of prices in his model, if indeed such a thing exists. (On a visit to Moscow, a Soviet mathematical economist complained of the absence of any model in Liberman's mind.) Ideas and proposals have come forward in infinite variety.

A whole long paper could be devoted to the efforts of the Central Mathematical Economics Institute in Moscow, their colleagues in Novosibirsk and to such men as Kornai and Liptak in Hungary[3]. Two-level or multi-level planning would, it is hoped, make possible the search for an optimum without an impossible overburdening of

---

[1] See his *Planning and the Market Under Socialism* (International Arts and Science Publications, New York, 1967; also published in Prague).

[2] *Plan i rynok* (Moscow, 1966).

[3] E.g. see J. Kornai and T. Liptak. 'Two-level planning', *Econometrica*, 1963.

the centre. There is also an increasing realisation that structure and motivation are integral parts of the problem. It may be worth mentioning in passing that the prewar Lange model of socialism never came to grips with motivation: *why* should socialist planners respond to the information they receive? Is it not simplest to do nothing rather than *tâtonner*? Western mathematically-inclined economists today show a remarkable predilection to ignore structure, as if the context within which a decision is taken, the area of responsibility of the individual taking it, did not affect resource allocation. Yet the boundary-line between internalities and externalities quite obviously does affect decisions, whether our textbooks and formulae recognise this or no. Since Soviet mathematical economists find themselves having to advise government about reform of management, they at least cannot allow themselves the luxury of disembodied abstraction, and I have met no *Soviet* mathematician who would look contemptuously down upon those who talk of institutions.[1] They have in fact set up 'laboratories' to research on optimal institutional and motivational structures.

Resistance and objective obstacles to change

It is widely believed that a fundamental reform of the Soviet system of planning was promulgated or began in 1965. This would be a quite misleading impression. There have, it is true, been a number of changes in the system of indicators and incentives. Management at plant level is freer in deciding the composition of its labour force (subject to keeping within the prescribed total of wages and salaries), it is no longer to receive binding plan-orders regarding gross value of output, or cost reduction, a wider range of minor investments can now be financed by the enterprise itself. In computing managerial bonuses profits play a bigger (though not the sole) role. Other changes include the introduction of a capital charge, payable by every enterprise to the state budget. This represents not only a departure from established habits, but also a recognition that subordinate units of management influence the orders they receive, and therefore that making capital more expensive would affect applications for investment finance and thereby the investment plans of the centre.

[1] How in fact can one have a theory of the firm without recognising that the firm is an institution, with a structure which affects its acts?

But the essentials of the old system have survived in the U.S.S.R.—though not in Hungary.

1. Planning of production and (within limits set by time and feasibility) of the product mix, is still within the province of the government organs.

2. Administrative allocation of inputs and products survives, with relatively few exceptions. Contractual relationships remain based on allocation certificates, which specify customers and suppliers.

3. Prices remain in principle as well as in practice unresponsive to demand and scarcity conditions. They are fixed by planning agencies or the government, and as a rule cannot be altered in negotiations.

4. Therefore profitability cannot in practice be used as a rational guide to resource allocation. The incentive system at enterprise level is immensely complicated, and in all cases of conflict between plan-orders and profitability the former has priority.

It is no part of the present argument to assert that the choice is either 100% centralization *or* a genuinely free market. Such perfect types exist nowhere. The fact remains that the management model in the U.S.S.R. is still, with exceptions relating mainly to detail and to procedure, very much what it was. The market, competition, an active role for prices, are not yet part of the accepted orthodoxy, and indeed in the present 'climate' some of the more radical proposals have ceased to appear in print.

Hungary is quite different. But before contrasting the two countries, we should dwell briefly on the obstacles which stand in the way of change. They are of several kinds:—

1. There is no agreed reform model. The political leadership is presented with many contradictory proposals.

2. The inadequacy of some (if not most) of the proposals. Thus Liberman ignores the important fact that many decisions and computations ought *not* to be made on the basis of profitability as seen at enterprise (plant) level. Were it otherwise, it would be hard to explain the existence of I.C.I., General Electric and other giant corporations, whose expansion presumably demonstrates the existence, in some fields at least, of organisational as well as technical economies of scale.

3. The fascinating work done by the mathematical school is not yet by any means applicable to national-economic optimal planning.

There are grave problems in the way of defining the objective function; what is it that one is optimising? In real-life situations, even a defined objective function is not enough. A chess game has a clear objective, that of winning in accordance with agreed rules. A chess-playing programme is none the less remarkably difficult to devise. It may be unnecessary to point out that a chessboard has only 64 squares and that the pieces obey clear rules. The simplest input-output table has many more squares than this, and the variety of human behaviour somewhat exceeds that of chessmen. It would be quite wrong to assert that a computerised optimising management structure has been devised, which political opposition is blocking.

4. Political-ideological opposition to reform does exist, of course. There is habit, inertia, bureaucratic vested interests, not unknown in western institutions (and indeed in universities!). Both the strictly 'political' and the upper managerial strata can easily become upset by the thought that they are no longer to issue binding orders on matters great and small. Some reformers' stress on market relations upset people accustomed to the notion that socialism is the substitution of deliberate choice by 'society' for the 'anarchic' market.

5. The very real problem of transition. The 'traditional' system was based on a logical principle: collection of information about needs was followed by instructions as to who is to meet what need. Under conditions of full utilisation of resources, with a tendency to excess demand, it is hard to make a *partial* change in the system. Thus to take one example: there has been an increase in the volume of decentralised investment; but decentralised investment is not planned, and so the the building materials and equipment which it required were not planned either. Therefore decentralised investments are often frustrated. The simplest way out is to put them back into the plan, i.e. to recentralise. Partial reform may prove self-defeating, radical and total reform is regarded as too risky.

6. The problem of monopoly has yet to receive a satisfactory solution. A recent trend in the U.S.S.R. has been the amalgamation of enterprises within the same field into so-called 'associations' (*obyedineniya*, perhaps 'Soviet corporations'). This development is consistent with the negative official view of intra-branch competition. But a monopolist instructed to maximise profits is unlikely to act in the public interest, in any system. Soviet critics have reminded us, for instance, that state retail stores show better financial results if

shoppers stand in queues. (Nor is the experience of British national-ised industries entirely satisfactory over the question of operational criteria.)

7. No one is yet clear as to what to do with unsuccessful enter-prises ('socialist bankruptcy'?). There is also fear of unemployment, and there is concern to reconcile regional policy with the use of rate-of-return as the criterion.

For all these reasons, the great firm U.S.S.R. Ltd. is still being managed in the old way, though with greater flexibility at the edges and a great deal of talk about change coming.

Hungary: a market model

The principles of the Hungarian reform are set out in the *Resolution of the Hungarian Workers'* (i.e. communist) *Party*. My English-language copy is undated, but it seems to have been adopted in 1966 and its introduction began in January 1968. A few quotations will highlight the differences between this approach and the Soviet.

1. 'A greater scope for competition between enterprises', to 'stimulate efficiency and satisfy the consumer'. There is emphasis throughout on 'the market'.

2. Enterprise managers shall be free to decide 'what and how much they want to produce and market', and 'from what enterprises and in what quantities they want to purchase (inputs) for their own money'.

3. While some prices would be controlled, prices would in prin-ciple be such as to balance supply and demand. 'The value-judgments of markets have to express themselves in prices'. 'Differentiation of profit should influence the shaping of demand and supply and help in bringing about the equilibrium of the market'.

4. Domestic and foreign prices are to be linked, via a realistic exchange rate, so that as soon as practicable the Hungarian pur-chaser is 'free to choose between domestic and imported goods', while the managers will be 'free to decide whether to sell on the domestic or foreign markets'. Foreign trade, of course, plays a much bigger role in the Hungarian than in the Soviet economy, and the decree specifically envisages the use of imports as an anti-monopoly device.

Major investment decisions, affecting 'the basic proportions' of the economy, remain in the hands of the central planners. They also have potent weapons, through taxes, exchange rates, import duties, price control, directives to the banks with regard to short and long-term credit, by which the behaviour of enterprise management can be influenced or circumscribed.

Not all these measures have been fully implemented, but Hungarian planning has dropped mandatory plan-orders for enterprises and has abandoned administrative allocation of resources in principle, and to a substantial extent also in practice. Only a few key production tasks still remain as administratively-determined priorities.

Compare this with the pronouncements of the chairman of the State Committee on Prices in Gosplan, Sitnin: 'Market prices are, in our view, alien to our economy and contradict the task of strengthening centralised planning. In our view it is also totally incorrect to imagine that prices must balance supply and demand, should increase in the event of shortage of this or that product . . . The balance between demand and supply is achieved by the proportional development of all parts of the economy and is the task of the planning organs.'[1]

Hungary's reform was preceded by an increase in stocks, so that price rises, which were widely feared, did not in fact follow the elimination of many price controls. A fascinating Soviet view of the whole process was recently published, where data are cited to the effect that prices actually fell,[2] though 'the operations of enterprises are determined principally by market forces'.

Managerial ingenuity can now be devoted to greater efficiency. Under the 'Soviet' system that existed in Hungary until 1958, managerial ingenuity was needed too, but for rather different purposes: 'how to find a way to employ five extra workers within a fixed wages fund . . . Now we have no such problem. We decide what wages fund is needed, how many workers we employ'.[3]

The Hungarian managers have to pay for new equipment, out of their own resources or on credit. This is contrasted by the Russian commentator with what happened in his country. 'Every year an enterprise would receive a sum from the state budget "for new technique". It spent the money without bothering to calculate. And why calculate? Last year they got this money, and this year, and no

[1] *Ekonomicheskaya gazeta*, No. 6, 1968, pp. 10–11.
[2] P. Volin. *Novyi mir*, No. 3, 1969, pp. 157–8.
[3] *Ibid.*, p. 159.

doubt next year they will get it. The one concern was to spend it. If any was left, the grant would be reduced next year, and maybe the manager will be reprimanded for not showing due concern with technical progress.'[1]

The Soviet writer finds occasion to extol the virtues of competition, by quoting the Hungarians. Is it a 'capitalist' word? Not at all, since it is precisely 'capitalist monopolies which throttle competition' in the west. Will there not be trouble for weaker enterprises? Certainly. The danger of real trouble is essential. 'The market must be a real, not a pseudo market. Otherwise we would have to return to administrative means of control. A real market must have competition.'

As these quotations show, the Soviet reader is being made aware of the contrast between the two countries. No doubt the Hungarian experience is being carefully studied in Moscow. It should also be carefully studied in the west.

Why the difference?

Why are Budapest and Moscow following different paths? We must not overlook the possibility that it is really the same path, with Moscow a few years behind, and indeed some Soviet economists, when I discussed these questions with them in 1967, argued along these lines: 'We are a great power, we cannot afford to take risks. Let the smaller states with fewer responsibilities make the mistakes, and we will learn from them.' However, on my visit to Moscow this year the economists were much less sure that the Soviet leadership has accepted even the principle of radical reform. It may be pushed into it later, but for the present they may feel that the cautious steps already taken represent as far as they can safely go.[2]

Why then, the difference? One argument introduced both in conversation and in the already-quoted article by Volin is that 'the U.S.S.R. is much bigger'. If by that is meant that the process of transition is more complex, this is logical enough. However, one of the principal arguments for the reformers is that the economy is too big to be effectively centralisable, and on this view it is the much smaller Hungarian economy which could continue to be run centrally.

[1] P. Volin. *Novyi mir*, No. 3, 1969 pp. 157–8.
[2] This view is quoted, without approval, by A. Birman in *Novyi mir* No. 12, 1968.

More serious is the view that the very much greater reliance of Hungary on foreign trade predisposed the economic leadership to a more 'liberal' view, and a strong case can be made out for the proposition that a closed[1] economy is easier to plan in the 'Stalin' manner. The typical Soviet exports are still 'bulk' items such as timber, grain, iron ore, oil, which can be effectively sold by a central agency. (Equipment is exported in the main under bilateral agreements, centrally negotiated.)

However, Poland and East Germany are almost as dependent on foreign trade as is Hungary, but have not adopted her 'market' approach. One is driven to political explanations.

One of these relates to what the Soviet economist Birman has called the 'psychological barrier'. New methods are resisted by those who have never known any but the old administrative planning system. Hungary, by contrast, only adopted the Soviet methods around 1950, and began to modify them cautiously after the shock of 1956. The priority given by the U.S.S.R. to the arms race may be relevant too.

More explicitly political is the view taken of the role of the Communist party in the economy. Historically this role fulfilled a vital purpose, that of transforming the economy and society. Given the aims of the regime in the first part of Stalin's reign, it would have been absurd to speak of a market-orientated plan; the object was to change by revolution from above all the ingredients which made up the market. But in the process the party (and the government officials whom the party appoints) has come to regard the issuance of orders as its special privilege. Indeed the top stratum's privileges depend on its control over the instruments of production and over distribution. It happens, among other things, to give them first claim on scarce resources (caviar and refrigerators among them) and also the authority to decide who should have them and other special advantages. The top management is a kind of oligarchy, which recruits by promotion through a system of establishment committees which, through the party machine, it controls. In the U.S.S.R. this system has been firmly established for decades, and has certain roots in Russian history.[2] The exercise of control by the party over

---

[1] Until recently, Soviet exports were a mere 3 % or less of GNP. Hungary's are closer to 30%.

[2] See A. Nove, 'History, hierarchy and nationalities; some observations on Soviet social structure', *Soviet Studies*, July, 1969.

management—or the exercise of supreme managerial functions by the party leadership—is so closely bound up with the whole social-political system that change is bound to be resisted strongly. The party in Hungary is weaker, and its attempt to achieve total dominance in society was rudely interrupted by the events of 1956. It has exerted power with care and restraint ever since, aware of its precarious position and not at all sure of its right to order managers (or anyone else) about.

Some conclusions

It has been suggested at the beginning of this paper that the distinction between political and economic is hard to draw, that many political leaders are also senior managers. History knows of instances of large territories being governed by boards of directors of corporations: the East India Company is the obvious example. There too it would be hard to draw the line between economic and political. Some would also argue that any western government spends much of its time dealing with economic issues. This is true, but in the Soviet system the political organs also manage and operate the whole economic-industrial machine, in a way and to an extent qualitatively different from the west. The distinction between political and economic may be seen in the fact that the heads of the nationalised fuel industries in this country do not hold government rank, whereas the equivalent of the Chairman of the National Coal Board in the U.S.S.R. is the Minister of Coal Industry.

In the U.S.S.R. today the purely 'political' economic decision is under criticism, labelled 'voluntarist'. Khrushchev was guilty of 'voluntarism'. Wisdom is equated with achieving the best results with minimum inputs. To the extent to which men holding ministerial or high party rank behave thus, they behave like managers. They act as the visible hand.

Of course there remain considerable elements of political and personal arbitrariness. The burden of the arms race, the high cost of keeping up with America, continues to introduce into the picture a degree of priority which strengthens traditional attitudes. But it remains useful to return to the image of U.S.S.R. Ltd., with the politbureau as its board of directors. Like all big and growing corporations, it finds that decision-making must be devolved. The separate units of which U.S.S.R. Ltd. is composed must increasingly

be allowed to make deals with one another, to reflect in their production the demands of customers without prior reference to head-
quarters. But such ideas seem to disrupt the customary patterns of
power and hierarchy. The directors enjoy power, do not take kindly
to an enlargement of the autonomy of their subordinates. Might it
not lead to distintegration, duplication, even chaos? Does not head-
quarters know best? Has not much been written in authoritative
books about concentration of capital and economies of scale? Is not
the centre responsible to the shareholders of the whole corporation,
whereas the managers of the bits cannot see the interest of the whole?

In the end, if and when an optimal managerial structure is discovered, it will doubtless show great variety. In some sectors the
advantages of free competition between relatively small management
units are doubtless overwhelming. In others control from the centre
appears advantageous. A clue could be obtained by studying the big
western corporations. These vary in the degree to which they feel able
to decentralise decision-making. A useful research project would be
to compare them in this respect (and in others) with a Soviet industrial ministry.

I have emphasised the formidable obstacles to radical change in
the U.S.S.R. However, change there will be. After all, the directors of
U.S.S.R. Ltd. want not only to maintain control, they also want
results, to increase their power in the world, and so they must seek
to reconcile their interests as super-managers with enhanced efficiency.

Finally, a few more general comments. It has often struck me that
economists insist on comparing Soviet irrationalities not with the real
troubles of a real western economy, but with a textbook model.
I have seen lengthy criticisms of Soviet investment criteria, for
instance. Yet a western manager facing a major investment decision,
say concerning a factory requiring four years to complete, must
make a guess at the following: wage rates in 1973, the prices of his
inputs and outputs in 1973, the behaviour of his competitors, the
rate of exchange, the rate of import duty at home or in foreign
markets, the future rate of interest, and a few other unknowns. It is
hardly self-evident that the net result is necessarily more rational
than Soviet investment decisions, with all their organisational and
pricing inadequacies.

The Soviet system of planning and management was devised to
transform an underdeveloped power into a modern industrial-
military state in a short period of time. It is still able to enlarge its

productive base rapidly, and it would be misleading to speak of crisis. None the less, the whole traditional pattern of ideas and structures is being questioned, and a slow and cautious attempt is being made to change the system to one more suitable to the needs of a diversified and sophisticated industrial economy.

Part II

Some Problems of Management

4

Short-term Forecasting for the U.K. Economy

James Shepherd*

This paper is concerned primarily with the methods currently used
(i.e. in September 1969) for short-term forecasting of the main
aggregates contributing to domestic economic activity. These forecasts are prepared as part of the background relevant to decisions on
central economic management. In a paper of this kind it is not
possible to discuss and defend in detail the way in which most of the
relationships involved have been handled, though one may look at
illustrative cases. It is hoped, however, that it may be possible to
describe the general approach adopted and to discuss some of the
major methodological issues. First, it should be emphasised that the
methods adopted depend on the context in which the work is carried
out; in particular on the results required, on the organisation within
which the forecasters are working, and on the resources available.

Objectives and organisation

The 'short-term forecasts' described here normally cover a period up
to some eighteen months to two years from the time of forecasting.
The continuation of existing Government policies, tax rates, etc. is
taken as an assumption. The 'key' results consist of quarter by
quarter projections of gross domestic product in real terms, of the
main components of final expenditure, total employment and unemployment, and cost and price movements. The forecasting exercise
is closely co-ordinated with a similar exercise covering balance of
payments movements, the resulting forecasts being consistent in all
respects.

The results are required in the first place, in aggregative national
accounting terms, and the main totals are disaggregated only in so
far as such treatment seems technically advantageous as a means of

* Senior Economic Adviser, H.M. Treasury.

obtaining the totals. More detailed work on the prospects for particular industries is carried out for its own sake rather than as a means of building up the aggregative forecasts, and draws on the aggregative demand forecasts. The consequences of the domestic forecast are also worked through into projections of income and expenditure at current prices, the financial balances of the main sectors of the economy and the flows of funds by which these balances are financed. These further projections are carried out by different forecasting teams from the preparation of the constant price demand forecasts and work is not completed until a little time after the constant price forecasts have been delivered.

Three main forecasting exercises are conducted each year, completion normally being in February, July and November. Each exercise involves the simultaneous presentation of a consistent set of domestic and balance of payments forecasts. In addition, various updating exercises are carried out in between the main forecasts to take account of the most recent developments, or of economic measures introduced by the Government. These exercises draw on the same forecasting relationships as the main forecasts but do not involve comprehensive reconsideration of parts of the forecast which there is no clear reason for changing. The idea of a continuously rolling forecast modified gradually from day to day, and therefore always up-to-date, has some obvious attractions. But it is possible that such a procedure might tend to inhibit more fundamental re-thinking and might actually tend to perpetuate assessments which no longer fitted the facts. Three times a year is perhaps as often as a relatively radical reconsideration is possible.

The forecasts are prepared by a working party representing the main economic departments. The Treasury takes the lead in organising the forecasting exercises and the forecasts are finally put together by a small group of economists and statisticians in the Treasury and the Central Statistical Office. However, officials from a number of other departments take the initiative on the subjects on which they have particular expertise, and also contribute their judgment to the crucial decisions affecting the forecasts as a whole.

The Construction of a Forecast

This section of the paper offers a general description of a forecast as it is now carried out. The exposition is deliberately unbalanced, dealing sketchily with some components of the forecast and in more detail with others: a more even treatment would lead either to a superficial account or to excessive length.

A very significant part of the forecasters' efforts is devoted to establishing the statistical basis of the forecast. This activity takes two main forms. First, the quarterly national accounting data may show erratic or inconsistent movements which require interpretation. And secondly there is a variety of statistical information not in national accounting form, which extends into a more recent period than the latest quarterly national accounts and which may be an alternative source of evidence about earlier periods.

The notion of a 'compromise' series for gross domestic product, obtained from the three largely independent estimates based on expenditure, incomes and output data, is by now fairly widely known.[1] As practised by Government forecasters the compromise is ultimately an average but some series are first smoothed and specific adjustments—e.g. for the effects of strikes—may be incorporated. For the two years or so running up to the start of a forecast a 'reconciled' expenditure series consistent with the compromise estimate of G.D.P. is compiled. The allocation of the necessary adjustments to components of expenditure is partly arbitrary—the stockbuilding figures bearing a good deal of the quarter to quarter adjustments—but is influenced by the forecasters' judgments as to the general plausibility of the picture presented. Compromise estimates of G.D.P. are compiled over a much longer period—though not necessarily at every forecasting round—as a prelude to the fitting of the various forecasting relationships. Broadly speaking the intention of the forecasters at this stage is to produce an estimate of 'what actually happened', even though this will include the effects of strikes, bad weather etc. which they do not reckon to forecast or to take directly into account in the forecasting relationships. A further stage in the forecasting process consists of making proper allowances for such disturbances in estimating and extrapolating the relationships. It may not always matter very much at which stage an adjustment is made: the intention is to present a recognisable picture of past history which reflects disturbances which everyone knows to have occurred. No comparable formal reconciliation is made of the income components of G.D.P.: but the forecasters take account of

[1] See W. A. H. Godley and C. Gillion, 'Measuring National Product', *National Institute Economic Review*, February, 1964.

discrepancies between income and compromise estimates when interpreting income movements.

The use of indicators for 'forecasting' the recent past is itself a major subject of research. For the quarter following that for which full national accounts are available there is usually a considerable amount of information on the expenditure side about imports, exports and personal consumption, on the output side about industrial production and on the incomes side about wage and salary earnings and retail prices. The figures for unemployment and vacancies which are available particularly quickly (monthly unemployment figures are published ten days after the count) are of value for their own sake but also reflect recent movements in economic activity. The extrapolation of national accounting series to reflect this evidence is somewhere between an art and a science. Where information is relatively complete it blends into the normal business of compiling national accounts statistics. An interesting account of the methods used by the Central Statistical Office in making preliminary estimates of personal consumption was recently published.[1]

I have given some stress to this backward-looking aspect of the forecast because I believe it to be important and because it does not receive a great deal of attention in academic circles.

The approach to the future is—in broad outline— a fairly conventional one. Relationships are sought which explain the development of the main categories of demand for goods and services and the extent to which they are met from home output or imports. While equations representing most of the relationships are in use, the forecast is not derived from a fully formalised model in the sense that there is a complete set of exogenous variables and equations which automatically lead to a solution.[2] In some cases, for reasons which will emerge, equations are not used: in others there is a variety of alternative equations and the final choice of forecast is a matter for discussion. In all cases where equations are used the forecasters use their judgment—bearing in mind recent experience and factors expected to operate over the forecast period—in projecting discrepancies from the equations which may differ from zero and which may change over time. The forecast is derived by an iterative process which eventually establishes consistency between the various

[1] 'Preliminary estimates of consumers' expenditure', *Economic Trends*, May 1969.
[2] Though a fully formalised model does exist. See para. commencing 'However . . .' on p. 74.

components of the forecast and the relationships by which they are estimated.

The first stage of the forecast involves meetings between the departments concerned to discuss components of the forecast which may be thought of as largely 'exogenous', in the sense that the outcome is not heavily dependent on the outcome for economic activity as a whole. No part of the forecast is wholly exogenous—even the public expenditure forecasts may have to be modified if the overall picture suggests a particularly severe load on (say) the construction industry: but it does assist the process of iteration if the less sensitive components such as public expenditure, exports and private fixed investment (which is clearly endogenous but with a fairly long time lag) can be taken first.

I do not intend to deal at any length with exports (which are the responsibility of the balance of payments forecasters) or with forecasts of public sector current expenditure and fixed investment. The public sector forecasts are based on financial year programmes and the relationship of these in the past to the outturn as recorded in the national accounts. These have to be tied in with known factors, such as delivery delays and supply shortages, and with the run of quarterly figures within the current financial year.

The treatment of private sector fixed investment (other than housing) has certain similarities to that of the public sector in that considerable weight is attached to information about spending plans —in this case via the Board of Trade's enquiries on investment intentions. However, revisions to plans in the light of economic circumstances can be important even within the period covered by a forecast. Therefore the more fundamental determinants of investment behaviour cannot be ignored. The treatment of private investment is a good example of a case where one single method such as might be incorporated in a formal model does not seem adequate; one must look at the situation from various angles and arrive at a judgment as to what seems a reasonable development (either as a 'central' figure or as a range) in all the circumstances. For instance, most people would agree that the important factors affecting cyclical developments in investment were changes in demand and capacity utilisation, expectations about future demand, the cost and availability of finance etc. But, given the possibilities for moods of optimism or pessimism, and given that large movements in a few firms or a small industry can have major effects on the national aggregates, there is no *a priori* reason for optimism about the possibility of obtaining 'structural' equations capable of making predictions with the order of accuracy (say within 5 per cent or so) that one is looking for in this kind of forecast. On the contrary, it would need impressive empirical evidence to convince one that this was the case. It is, no doubt, usually possible by exhaustive computation to produce an equation with distributed lags which provides a good fit to the last two or three cycles—and a little ingenuity will usually find a respectable theory to match it. But this, in the absence of convincing proof by extrapolation of comparable relationships fitted to earlier periods, is insufficient. However, intentions data also have their limitations: while they have been a very useful guide to the first year of a forecast they give less indication for the second: the degree of 'bias' in the estimates supplied by respondents has probably varied over time; and it is clear that the surveys have sometimes failed to anticipate changes in investment plans brought about by sharp changes in the trend of demand.

It is fairly clear, therefore, that a forecaster cannot afford to ignore either the evidence concerning intentions or the need for a 'causal' interpretation of past and prospective movements. Equally there may be obviously relevant factors, such as changes in the tax system, aspects of the monetary situation or changes in the structure of demand which may confront a forecaster on a particular occasion without there being appropriate past experience on which to base a statistical analysis. It seems fairly clear that in these circumstances the 'reasonable forecaster' has to put forward a figure (or range) on the basis of what is—to an important extent—a subjective judgment. This will also take into account other 'forward looking indicators' such as orders statistics, replies to C.B.I. surveys, etc.

The above remarks apply, primarily, to manufacturing investment, though many of the same considerations are relevant to the distributive and service industries. For these industries it is even harder than in the case of manufacturing to construct meaningful models relating capital stock to output, etc. but, fortunately, for this group (from which shipping is normally excluded) cyclical fluctuations have been somewhat smaller. Forecasts rely heavily on intentions data and the extrapolation of trends plus the assumption of some lagged response to economic and financial conditions.

For housing investment in the private sector somewhat different methods are used. While there are intentions data here as well (relating to the number of starts foreseen by builders) experience does not suggest that these are a very strong basis for forecasting. Moreover, attempts to predict short-term demand movements on the basis of developments in personal incomes have not achieved great success. There is therefore something of a gap in forecasting technique at this point. (The past history of starts is a useful forward indicator of the rate of investment in the earlier part of a forecast period.) On the other hand, rather more progress has been made towards a quantitative treatment of financial influences than in other parts of the forecasts. There are some occasions on which it may be reasonable to suppose that finance is not a constraint on housing investment and others on which it plainly is a constraint. Analysis by the Ministry of Housing and Local Government has made it possible to make approximate predictions of the number of sales of new houses which can be financed: this involves predictions of the inflow of funds into building societies taking into account the relative levels of the societies' and competitors' borrowing rates, the supply of funds from sources other than building societies and the proportion of funds allocated to new housing.

Forecasts of stockbuilding are more closely dependent than those of fixed investment on forecast developments in the economy as a whole. The basic hypothesis behind the forecasts is some type of 'stock adjustment' model in which there is a desired ratio of industrial stocks to output towards which stockholders tend to adjust; unforeseen changes in demand may, on the other hand, cause the actual ratio to shift away from the desired one. In this field, as in others, considerable attention is devoted to making appropriate adjustments for the effects of special factors such as strikes or the temporary import charge. The forecasts are not at present based on any particular equation (though a fair number have been estimated) but on a more general appraisal of the possible interpretations.

It is in the field of personal incomes and consumption (and also perhaps, employment and unemployment) that it has proved helpful to go relatively far towards formalisation of the forecasting procedure. For several of the key relationships there is a single 'guideline' equation which represents the main line of approach; but this still leaves room for looking at other approaches and for interpreting the error term. The main links in the chain of reasoning go through personal disposable incomes and prices to real disposable incomes and thence through consumer credit and savings to personal consumption.

Despite difficulties in relating nationally negotiated minimum rates to actual earnings, the statistical record still favours building up a forecast of wages and salaries—at least for the first year of a forecast—by first forecasting the index of hourly wage-rates. This enables the forecasters to draw on the detailed knowledge of the Department of Employment and Productivity concerning the course of claims and settlements, the working of incomes policy etc. It is necessary to make special adjustments in cases where the effect on earnings is not expected to be measured accurately by the movement of the wage index (where settlements are intended to affect only minimum earnings levels, for example). The guideline relationship currently in use relates wage and salary earnings per employee to hourly wage rates, to output in relation to 'capacity' (reflecting the extent of overtime and piecework earnings) and to a time-trend reflecting the historical fact that earnings have risen proportionately faster than wage rates. One version of this equation also allows the extent of 'wage-drift' to be influenced by the pressure of demand, but this coefficient is not statistically very well determined.

Current grants to persons and national insurance contributions are forecast on the basis of projections made by the Government Actuary and of other data incorporated in public expenditure forecasts: it is necessary to ensure that the unemployment assumption is consistent with the outcome of the forecast.

The remainder of the personal income account is not formalised though equations exist which help to form a view on company profits and hence on dividends. The remaining items such as self-employment incomes and miscellaneous interest receipts (net of payments) are forecast on the basis of the general situation, past trends and the effects of known special factors. The evidence does not show any clear relationship between net interest receipts and rates of interest; it may be that interest payments by the personal sector (e.g. on bank advances and mortgages) though smaller in amount than receipts are more rapidly sensitive to changes in interest rates.

Forecasts of consumer prices have been the subject of extensive econometric work[1] but still present considerable difficulties. Apart from issues relating to the appropriate theory of price formation there are difficult statistical problems in estimating lag structure under conditions where a fairly dispersed distributed lag is to be

[1] See W. A. H. Godley and D. A. Rowe, 'Retail and consumer prices', *National Institute Economic Review*, November 1964.

expected and where there is high auto-correlation of residuals. From the point of view of forecasting personal consumption the ultimate objective must be the appropriate currently weighted price deflator. However, this is approached via the retail price index for which forecasts are also required for their own sake. This index has the advantage of reflecting 'pure' price movements (unaffected by changes in composition) and is fairly easily broken down into categories appropriate to analysis and forecasting. Given a forecast of the retail price index the degree of correlation is sufficient to permit a reasonably confident translation into a forecast of the consumer price deflator: but adjustments for compositional effects are sometimes needed.

Most prices are assumed to be determined by costs—primarily wages and employers' contributions and import prices, with appropriate adjustment for indirect taxation. No pressure of demand variable has been found helpful, but the estimate of wage cost is a 'trend cost' variable which does not fall below trend in the cyclical upswing because of a temporarily accelerated growth in output per employee: a similar result might well be obtained using actual cost per unit of output and a positive pressure of demand coefficient. Retail prices for housing, nationalised industries and the largely supply-determined 'seasonal food' group are forecast outside the main econometric relationships using information from the departments concerned. The income forecast is then divided by the consumer price index to give a forecast of 'real personal disposable income'. In addition to income movements changes in consumer credit are brought in directly as determinants of consumption. Movements in debt outstanding reflect both demand for durable goods and policy measures affecting the terms on which hire purchase credit can be obtained and the availability of bank advances to persons. In the case of cars, forecasts of total spending on cars are linked with forecasts of new hire-purchase credit on cars and thence, via repayments, to net borrowing by consumers.

The consumption function relates the volume of consumption to three separate categories of real disposable income (wages and salaries, current grants and other income) and to net changes in consumer debt. Both the ultimate effect on consumption and the time lag before this is realised may vary for these four variables; the appropriate coefficients are subjected to *a priori* restrictions where free calculation of regression coefficients gives implausible answers. Other factors, such as capital gains and losses or expectations of price changes may be taken into account more impressionistically.

The consumption forecast completes the forecast of final expenditure. This has involved assumptions about the outcome for gross domestic product which may change when the circle has been completed by the forecasts of imports and the adjustment to factor cost. Hence the need for iteration.

Forecasts of imports consistent with the forecasts of final expenditure again come from the balance of payments team; they use a combination of regression methods relating certain major categories of imports (such as industrial materials, capital goods, etc.) to the appropriate components of the demand forecasts and an approach drawing on the expertise of departments on the situation relating to particular commodities. While an aggregate relationship between the volume of imports of goods and services and the components of final expenditure exists, it is used mainly to make quick adjustments when variations on a main forecast are required and as a rough check for consistency rather than as a means of reaching the main import forecast.

Forecasts of employment and unemployment are derived principally from aggregative relationships involving the volume of G.D.P. and the demographic determinants of the working population[1,2]. As with most formal relationships performance is apt to be less good in extrapolation than the assumption of stable relationships would warrant: judgments are frequently required as to why actual experience has diverged and may be expected to diverge from the relationships.

Some major issues

While the foregoing description was, in many respects, no more than an outline it is probably more profitable to elaborate by discussing some of the main technical issues and problems rather than to load on more detail concerning precisely what is done at each stage of the forecasting process.

[1] W. A. H. Godley and J. R. Shepherd. 'Long-term growth and short-term policy', *National Institute Economic Review*, August 1964.
[2] J. R. Shepherd. 'Productive potential and the demand for labour', *Economic Trends*, August 1968.

Monetary factors in the forecasts

In view of current interest in the role of monetary factors in influencing the course of the economy it may be helpful to review their treatment in the preparation of forecasts. References have already been made at appropriate points, but there are two main threads that should be drawn together. First, although there are some monetary influences which can be taken as exogenous to the forecasting system—in particular international monetary conditions and assumptions about U.K. policies—there are other factors which emerge more clearly when a forecast has been completed. For instance, in assessing the way in which financial conditions influence private investment and stockbuilding, it is helpful to take into account not only the appropriate policy variables but the pattern of flows of funds between sectors which would be required and the problems which might be experienced in achieving these flows, given the past pattern of flows and asset preferences. But these movements can only be estimated in the light of a complete national income and sectoral financing forecast. So we are faced with the familiar problem of interdependence. Conceptually, there is no problem; given the relationships determining both 'real' and 'monetary' events these can be integrated into a single model to be solved simultaneously. In practice, there is a long way to go before such comprehensive treatment can be achieved, though projections of sector financing are made and are required for their own sake as well as for their influence on the demand forecasts.

Secondly, it must be accepted that economists know comparatively little about how in detail monetary influences should be incorporated into relationships designed to forecast real demand. Apart from the usual problems of measurement and estimation there is a very wide area of doubt as to how particular relationships should be specified. For instance, there is often doubt concerning whether the important factor is the level of interest rates or the availability of credit from particular sources and as to how external credit conditions should be expected to relate to internal cash flows. There is also a strong presumption that many relationships are highly non-linear: this may reduce the chances of satisfactory estimates of parameters from limited data. There are some aspects, such as housing finance, in which progress has been made towards a more systematic treatment: in others the difficulties of obtaining valid econometric results still seem great.

The degree of formalisation

A long-standing controversy on forecasting methods concerns the relative merits of a completely formal and explicit 'model' at one extreme and a largely unexplained and subjective 'judgmental' approach at the other. It is fairly widely recognised by now that there is a more or less continuous spectrum of alternatives between these extremes. It will be clear from this paper that official forecasters take an intermediate position. Whilst econometrically estimated equations play a major part in the forecasts, the forecasting process does not consist simply of the application of a 'model' in the sense that the forecast is determined by substitution into a previously decided set of equations. In some cases the forecasters experiment with the implications of several alternative equations, in others there are none which seem helpful. In all cases where there are formal relationships it is necessary to try to interpret discrepancies from them—particularly in the most recent past—in terms of possible instability or incomplete specification. In the light of such analysis it will often be necessary to forecast a time series for the error term in that equation. Where a forecaster strikes the balance between formal and informal methods will depend partly on temperament and judgment and partly on external circumstances. While additional research and improved statistics may gradually make it possible to formulate and test more sophisticated relationships and to replace vague judgments by explicit equations there would seem to be no prospect of moving into a world in which such relationships are wholly stable over time or in which situations without adequate precedent do not occur. It is not, therefore, sensible to suppose that forecasting can be reduced to a wholly 'objective' activity, though a completely formalised simultaneous model may well be a useful tool.

Similar considerations apply to the choice of methods of estimation. In many cases the relationships required for forecasting involve explanatory variables which are endogenous to the system as a whole, leading to bias in coefficients estimated by single-equation least squares techniques. This may well be the case even when only lagged endogenous variables are involved, since there are seldom grounds for assuming that the error terms are not serially correlated.

Equally, it may often be necessary to assume broadly distributed lags of a type which are very difficult to estimate from limited data when serial correlation is to be expected. It may be of little comfort to possess consistent estimating techniques when the data consist of small samples. Given the enormous uncertainty as to what assumptions can reasonably be made, and the limited technical resources available, official forecasters have tended to lean heavily on the relative simplicity of ordinary least squares—a technique which does seem to be relatively robust in practice. It is, of course, necessary to treat the results critically according to the economic sense that they make, and to be particularly on the look-out for cases of serious bias introduced by single-equation techniques. It is certainly intended that the practical implications of using different estimating techniques should be more fully explored. As longer runs of quarterly national income data become available the relative advantages of using simultaneous equation methods may well increase; it cannot, however, be taken for granted that relationships will remain stable over the whole period for which data are available.

It should also be emphasised that estimation of the parameters in forecasting equations by time series analysis alone is not always the most appropriate technique, given the very wide margins of error which may be involved. It is often useful to take account of estimates based on, for example, ratios obtained from national accounts or input-output tables. For instance, the *average* import content of (say) consumers' expenditure or the relative weights of wages and import prices in total costs can be estimated tolerably accurately in this way. Debatable assumptions are involved in assuming that these estimates are those appropriate at the margin for use in forecasting equations. But this is true of almost all assumptions involved in specifying a model, and there are occasions on which these particular assumptions seem to be a lesser evil than the hazards of time series estimation. Official forecasters make considerable use of coefficients obtained from cross section data in this way.

Research and development

It is possible that the preceding remarks suggested a negative and sceptical attitude to the value of further research and the use of more refined statistical techniques. This was not intended. While we should not pre-suppose that lasting and complete answers are to be obtained, there is certainly a great deal more which can be done. It may be of interest to indicate some of the main directions in which research is being conducted within the Treasury; this is not, of course, a complete catalogue of work relevant to short-term forecasting proceeding within Government departments.

It is not easy, in the case of the operational team, to distinguish new research from up-dating of the system to take account of new evidence. New or revised figures may often tip the balance between the use of a relationship in one form rather than another, so that revision is seldom confined to the re-estimation of a single equation. One has to run quite hard to stay in the same place. Where possible, in the course of bringing the system up-to-date, old hypotheses are re-considered and new ones are examined: this may or may not involve a fundamental overhaul of existing procedures. Relatively radical re-thinking is now going on in the field of price-determination and stockbuilding for example.

However, it is also necessary to step back and look at the system as a whole. Is it possible to use advanced statistical techniques to cope more effectively with problems of estimation and interdependence? Can computer technology be applied to speeding up the forecasting procedure, and to a more thorough working through of the iterative process? While retaining the scope for human judgment is regarded as of paramount importance the major development work now in progress is in the field of computerisation. The present approach is to build a model as similar as possible to the less formal process used operationally: that is to select from existing equations, where these are available, and to develop others which resemble as closely as possible the more informal lines of reasoning used in other cases. Certain components of demand such as public expenditure and exports clearly have to remain exogenous at this stage. With the aid of consultants a program for solving this model, and presenting the output in convenient tabular form, has been drawn up and the staff and facilities to keep this in operational form are being acquired.

It will be clear from the paper so far that the objective is not simply to feed in the data and imagine that a good forecast will come straight out. Exactly how the model will be subsumed into the forecasting process will depend on experience. Initially, the intention is to conduct the main forecast by existing procedures and to use the model mainly for calculating the implications of different assumptions either about policy or about the outcome of some particular component. Once a main forecast is obtained the system can readily be solved for the implied residual errors and these can be retained—or modified in specific ways—when the system is re-solved on the alternative assumption. This provides a good way of providing rapid estimates of the effects of policy changes (or equally of, say, a different outcome for exports) which take relatively full account of the interdependence of the economic system.

However, such a model will also provide a research tool which will, presumably, in the longer term affect the method of making a main forecast. It should be particularly helpful in exploring the implications for the forecast as a whole of different approaches in any one part of the system, and as a structural basis underlying the application of simultaneous-equation estimation techniques.

Bibliography

'Short-term economic forecasting in the United Kingdom.' *Economic Trends,* August 1964.
'Measuring national product,' by W. A. H. Godley and C. Gillion. *National Institute Economic Review,* February 1964.
'Long-term growth and short-term policy' by W. A. H. Godley and J. R. Shepherd. *National Institute Economic Review,* August 1964.
'Retail and consumer prices,' by W. A. H. Godley and D. A. Rowe. *National Institute Economic Review,* November 1964.
Techniques of Economic Forecasting, O.E.C.D., 1965.
'An analysis of tax changes,' by W. A. B. Hopkin and W. A. H. Godley. *National Institute Economic Review,* May 1965.
Fourth Report from the Estimates Committee, Session 1966–67, on Government Statistical Services (HMSO, December 1966), pp. xxx–xxxii, 34–48, 438–446, and 474–480.
'Econometric research for short-term forecasting.' *Economic Trends,* February 1967.
'Short-term forecasting of United Kingdom exports,' by M. C. Fessey. *Economic Trends,* May 1967.
'Short-term forecasts of income, expenditure and saving,' by L. S. Berman and F. Cassell. *Economic Trends,* February 1968.
'Productive potential and the demand for labour,' by J. R. Shepherd. *Economic Trends,* August 1968.
'The short-term effects of tax changes,' by J. R. Shepherd and M. J. C. Surrey. *National Institute Economic Review,* November 1968.
'Preliminary estimates of consumers' expenditure.' *Economic Trends,* May 1969.

5

Monetary Policy

Peter M. Oppenheimer*

I. The Nature of Monetary Policy

Monetary policy is the oldest form of macro-economic management. Historically it first appeared as control of the coinage. Every schoolboy learns how mediaeval kings resorted periodically to clipping or debasing the coins in order to pay for military and other extravagances. Such debasement was the forerunner of the printing press as a means of allowing governments to pre-empt real resources. Subsequently the debased coinage might be called in and re-minted at full weight—a 'currency reform' as we should designate it now.

Needless to say, the objectives of monetary policy and the framework in which it operates have become rather more complex than in the Middle Ages. Monetary policy is now seen chiefly as a means of controlling aggregate domestic demand. In this it works jointly with fiscal policy, though in many countries—Britain not among them— it plays the major role because fiscal policy is too inflexible. The aim is to preserve full employment combined with reasonable price stability. Balance-of-payments equilibrium has also to be maintained, at least in the medium term, but this may require resort to other, 'expenditure-switching' weapons, such as the exchange rate. So far as monetary policy is concerned, attention has to be paid to the direct impact of interest rates on international capital movements, as well as to the indirect effects of monetary measures on the external balance via aggregate demand.

This set of objectives is post-Keynesian in character. Before Keynes the emphasis was not on aggregate demand and employment but on the nominal value of money (which, admittedly, in some not very clear way, was supposed to affect the general economic situation). The shibboleth that emerged from the classical central-banking

* Student of Christ Church, Oxford.

tradition of the nineteenth century was 'internal and external stability of the currency'. This slogan sidestepped the fact that the two kinds of stability—stability of domestic prices and stability of the exchange rate—might be incompatible; but when a clash between them appeared, a theoretically 'sound' policy demanded priority for the exchange rate. This was particularly so in the United Kingdom, where the gold standard was associated with Britain's rise to financial and economic (as well as political) pre-eminence. Her dominant position in the international economy as trader and lender helped to prevent any serious disequilibrium in her balance of payments in the fifty years before 1914. Thus, the responsiveness of international capital movements to changes in short-term interest rates was the major and almost the only rationale of U.K. monetary policy, and the Bank of England continued to operate on this premise until 1931.[1]

As regards the framework in which monetary policy operates, the essential feature of domestic monetary systems in the twentieth century is that they are based on credit rather than commodity money. Money consists of bankers' liabilities, banknotes being the liabilities of the central bank, deposits of the commercial banks. Matching these liabilities are bankers' assets, mostly claims either on the government or on private businesses and individuals.[2] Monetary policy operates on the size and composition of the banks' balance sheets, with a corresponding impact on the balance sheets (real or notional) of the non-bank public.

---

[1] It may also be pointed out that from 1945 until the mid-1960s Bank of England policy on currency matters was more or less dominated by the idea of promoting the international role of sterling. After 1950 the Bank was hostile to the European Payments Union and was constantly pressing for a return to convertibility. It achieved this *de facto* in February 1955, though it was not formalised until December 1958. As late as April 1962 the Bank, in its Memorandum to the Halsbury Committee on decimal currency, gave the preservation of sterling's international role as the crucial reason for retaining the pound in a decimal currency system. Less has been heard of such arguments since then.

Both the Bank and the Treasury were extraordinarily wooden in dealing, or rather not dealing, with the problem of 'diversification' of the overseas sterling area's reserves during the 1960s. Basically, their policy was to ignore it. They did this even after the devaluation of November 1967—until the movement out of sterling balances reached such dimensions that they were forced to take action during 1968. They were then saddled with the Basle Arrangement of September 1968, a bad bargain from Britain's point of view, which more timely action would have made unnecessary.

[2] Central-bank assets, of course, still include some gold (or occasionally silver).

For example, suppose the authorities are trying to reduce spending by contracting the stock of money. The textbook procedure is for the central bank to make an open-market sale of government paper from its portfolio to the non-bank public. This first of all reduces the total of the central bank's own balance sheet, while among the non-bank public financial investors are induced to shift (directly or indirectly) from cash to government debt. The commercial banks are affected by the withdrawal of cash to pay for the government debt. Their deposit liabilities and their cash reserves at the central bank ('bankers' deposits') fall by equal amounts, reducing their reserve ratios and putting them under pressure to contract their lending in order to restore the reserve ratio. This is the familiar bank-credit multiplier. Contraction will continue until the money stock has declined by

$$S. \frac{1}{r+n-rn}$$

where S is the original open-market sale, r the banks' reserve ratio and n the public's currency-to-total-money ratio.[1] The decline in bank deposits will be the fraction $(1 - n)$ of the total. As the public's money balances fall, its expenditure on goods and services is supposed to fall also because it is now unwilling or unable to finance expenditure at the previous level.

Up to four different effects of tight money can contribute to this result. First, the higher interest rates necessary to persuade the public to part with some of its cash may make certain expenditures, especially on long-lived investments or on consumer durables, seem no longer worthwhile. Secondly, some outlays will be frustrated by credit-rationing or 'availability' effects, reflecting the imperfection of the credit and capital markets. The Radcliffe Report ten years ago placed considerable emphasis on this point for both bank and non-bank credit.[2] Thirdly, the fall in security prices (including equities) may reduce spending through 'wealth effects', besides contributing to

---

[1] It is assumed in the foregoing analysis that the public's currency ratio remains unchanged, an assumption not always wholly justified. If this ratio rises the monetary squeeze is intensified; if it falls the squeeze is mitigated.

[2] *Committee on the Working of the Monetary System*, Cmnd 827, HMSO 1959. The Committee referred particularly to the 'stickiness' of interest rates in institutions such as building societies, which caused these institutions to be squeezed for funds in periods of rising market rates.

credit rationing through the lowered value of pledgeable assets.[1] Finally, the psychological impact of tight money and higher interest rates may be to make both businessmen and consumers draw in their horns a little and become more cautious about major investment outlays. The psychological impact may be weakened by expectations that the credit squeeze will be short-lived; but the interest-rate and wealth effects will be strengthened by this.

So much for the textbook model of monetary policy—which also applies *mutatis mutandis* for a monetary expansion. The following two sections discuss some of its practical limitations. We look first at obstacles to controlling the quantity of money, with particular reference to recent British experience, and then at the link between the quantity of money and expenditure. The fourth section considers certain alternative techniques of monetary control and their validity, and a final section lists some brief conclusions.

II. Obstacles to Controlling the Quantity of Money

Open-market operations are obviously not a feasible method of conducting monetary policy if bill and bond markets are non-existent or too thin. In that case other techniques must be used, such as changes in the banks' reserve requirements or control of their foreign position.[2] In the United Kingdom, however, the Bank of England has long maintained that open-market operations are impossible not because the securities markets are too bad but because they are too good, and the Bank's first duty is to keep them that way. Its view, fully set out in its *Quarterly Bulletin* for June 1966, is that, in order to maximise the long-run demand for British government debt, it must guarantee 'for practical purposes, limitless marketability' of such debt. In other words, if the public wants to sell, the Bank must buy and without lowering prices too quickly. This, of course, is a recipe for paralysing any attempt to squeeze the money supply in the short run, since financial investors will naturally tend to sell government stocks if they expect the price to go on falling.

---

[1] Some recent econometric research in the United States has found wealth effects on private consumption to be quite large. See F. de Leeuw and E. M. Gramlich, 'The Channels of Monetary Policy', *Federal Reserve Bulletin*, June 1969.

[2] This last method has been practised by several continental countries in the 1960s. For an account of some of the episodes see A. I. Bloomfield, 'Forward exchange intervention: some recent experiences', *Banca Nazionale del Lavoro Quarterly Review*, 1964.

If the Bank's arguments were right, there would be a conflict between short-run and long-run objectives of policy. However, the Bank's view is implausible *a priori* and unsupported by evidence. Where large investors want to provide for liquidity at short notice they will not in any case hold bonds, however marketable; and for smaller transactions some market in gilt-edged can always be made without the Bank's participation. As to evidence, the figure of *minus* £95m. for net market sales of government stock over the five fiscal years 1964–69 speaks for itself. Government financing needs were acute during this period, but were met entirely by the external deficit and the expansion of the money supply. The arguments of the Bank appear to be little more than a rationalisation of its penchant for 'orderly markets' and its reluctance to push long-term interest rates up.

Economists in the past have not failed to make these points[1], and since 1968 pressure from the International Monetary Fund has led to a new emphasis on changes in the quantity of money (or 'Domestic Credit Expansion', which is a kind of *ex ante* change in the money stock, before the balance-of-payments deficit or surplus has affected the outcome)[2] and to a consequent shift of policy in the gilt-edged market. In the year ending May 1969 gilt-edged yields were allowed to rise by two full points from $7\frac{1}{2}$ to $9\frac{1}{2}\%$. However, the Bank of England continued to purchase large amounts of stock from the market during this period, and in its public pronouncements insisted that the change was a purely tactical one, indicating no basic change of priorities.[3] Its longer-run importance cannot yet be assessed.

While the Bank's line is easy to criticise, the difficulties facing it

[1] See, for example, A. K. Cairncross, *Monetary Policy in a Mixed Economy*, Wicksell Lectures, Stockholm, 1960; or D. J. Coppock and N. J. Gibson, 'The volume of deposits and the cash and liquid assets ratios', *Manchester School*, 1963. One notices, however, that economists who have spent some time in the Bank are more sympathetic to its point of view. Thus, for example, A. B. Cramp, 'The control of bank deposits', *Lloyds Bank Review*, October 1967; and A. D. Bain, 'Monetary policy', in A. R. Prest Ed. *Public Sector Economics*, Manchester U.P., 1968.

[2] See *Economic Trends*, May 1969, and *Bank of England Quarterly Bulletin*, September 1969. A succinct analysis of liquidity creation and absorption in several major countries may be found in the Annual Reports of the Netherlands Bank, beginning in 1963; see the section entitled 'Monetary trends in a number of countries'.

[3] *Bank of England Quarterly Bulletin*, March 1969, pp. 15–16.

in the later 1960s must not be underrated. Britain's national debt remains far larger in relation to GNP than that of any other major country—about 90%—and refinancing problems are continuous. More important, from 1964 until 1968 monetary policy had to contend with a massive budget deficit. The view has been propounded that 1966–68 was a period in which fiscal restraints failed to operate because monetary policy was so lax[1], but this view lacks foundation. The impression of fiscal restraint is probably due to our custom of emphasising the revenue side of government finance in the annual budget speech, to the near-exclusion of the expenditure side.[2] Certainly a lot of taxes have gone up in recent years, but public outlays were rising so fast until late in 1968 that revenue barely kept pace. The public sector's financial position for the period was as follows:

Table 1: *Deficit or Surplus of the Public Sector, 1964–69*

	1964	1965	1966	1967	1968	1969
			(£m.)			
Central and local government	− 428	− 747	+ 49	− 627	− 302	− 367
Public corporations	− 581	− 101	− 841	− 1044	− 736	+ 691
Total	− 1009	− 848	− 792	− 1671	− 1038	+ 324

Source: *Preliminary Estimates of National Income and Balance of Payments, 1964–69*, Cmnd 4328.

A few comments are in order on the interpretation of these figures. First, it is the yearly changes in the financial position which are relevant, rather than its level. In this connection it may be recalled that 1964 was the year of Mr. Maudling's pre-election boom. The figures indicate some tightening in 1965–66, followed by a substantial easing the following year and a much larger re-tightening in 1969.

Secondly, the figures *understate* the expansionary impact of the public sector during this period, because realised tax receipts were

[1] See, for instance, A. A. Walters, *Money in Boom and Slump*, Hobart Paper No. 44, London, 1968. In subsequent correspondence Professor Walters wrote to me: 'I would regard the 1966 budget as being tough, the 1967 budget as not easing the situation, and the devaluation budget of 1967 and the 1968 budget have been even more tough'. Later, in "Money supply and the gilt-edged market", *The Banker*, November 1969, Professor Walters took a more cautious line.

[2] A point to which Samuel Brittan draws attention in *Steering the Economy*, London, 1969, ch. 3, p. 65.

boosted by the strong demand situation for which the steep rise in public spending was itself largely responsible.[1] Public sector spending on goods, services and capital formation at current prices rose by 43% from 1964 to 1968, while GNP rose by 24%. The share of these items in GNP went up from 27·9 to 31·3%. This point is offset to a slight extent by two other facts. First, about one-third of the growth in public sector outlays consisted of transfer payments (National Insurance, other personal grants, debt interest and subsidies), a small part of which—probably under 5%—may have been saved rather than spent by the recipients. Secondly, the recession in the first half of 1967 was due not only to U.K. financial policy but also to an autonomous deterioration in the balance of payments on current account. This reflected the short recessions in Germany and the United States (hence slower growth of U.K. exports) and the removal of the U.K. import surcharge in November 1966 (hence faster growth of imports). The impact of this on the U.K. budget was to reduce tax receipts and thus worsen the budget outturn relative to the estimates. These qualifications, however, are not sufficient to upset the main conclusion. Fiscal policy fluctuated during the period, but was not markedly restrictive until the end of 1968. In these circumstances monetary restraint was bound to be an uphill struggle.

A further possible obstacle to controlling the quantity of money is the international mobility of liquid capital. This has undoubtedly been a headache for policy in some countries. In 1960, most notably, the German Bundesbank's efforts to curb a domestic boom through credit restraint and the Federal Reserve's efforts to bring the U.S. economy out of recession by means of cheap money were both largely frustrated by a massive flow of funds from America to Europe. The episode was a reminder that in a system of fixed exchange rates and substantial mobility of capital the international repercussions of monetary measures cannot be ignored—for domestic no less than balance-of-payments reasons.[2]

---

[1] For a formula which aims to measure the impact of the public sector in a comprehensive way see Richard A. and Peggy B. Musgrave, 'Fiscal Policy', in R. E. Caves and Associates, *Britain's Economic Prospects* (Brookings Institution 1968).

[2] These problems have also been more fully investigated in the theoretical literature of the 1960s, particularly by Robert A. Mundell. See his *International Economics*, New York, 1968.

Central banks have now become quite sophisticated in dealing with them—see, for example, the article by Bloomfield listed in footnote 2 on p. 79.

In Britain, however, the problem has been rather slight. Address-
ing the British Association two years ago, Professor A. D. Bain took
a more serious view of it. He pointed out that

'An increase in net liabilities to overseas at times of strong
demand for funds in the U.K. has made a substantial contribution
to the total funds available to the U.K. private sector at such
times. In the absence of these funds domestic interest rates would
certainly have been higher, and some potential borrowers would
have gone without funds.'[1]

This may perhaps be true, but it is not the same as saying that the
inflows from overseas frustrated attempts to squeeze credit at home,
for that depends on whether the authorities were in fact trying to
squeeze credit at the time.

The two main channels for the overseas borrowing in question
have been (a) sterling deposits made by non-residents with local
authorities and hire-purchase finance companies, and (b) the
'swapping' of foreign-currency deposits into sterling, either by
London banks (who in turn usually deposit the proceeds with local
authorities or hire purchase companies) or by U.K. business firms.
There were two spells during sterling's period of weakness in the
later 1960s when these channels brought a net inflow of funds to the
United Kingdom. In the eighteen months ending June 1965 some
£300m. was obtained; and in the first half of 1967 some £160m.[2]
Except for the first six months of 1965, however, these were not
periods when the authorities were trying to enforce credit restraint.
Indeed, in the first half of 1967 they were trying positively to ease it;
Bank rate was reduced in three stages from 7 to $5\frac{1}{2}\%$ and the 105%
ceiling on clearing bank advances was lifted. As to the first half of
1965, it is fair to say that credit restraint was a half-hearted policy, at
any rate until the call for Special Deposits at the end of April. The
newly arrived Labour Government had rejected what it called 'a
return to stop-go economics', and was more concerned with protect-
ing the reserves. It is noteworthy that the policy of supporting the
forward-exchange rate, which was a crucial factor in the continued

---

[1] A. D. Bain, loc. cit., pp. 172–3.
[2] The £300m. figure slightly overstates the true inflow, at least from a balance-of-
payments point of view, because there was some switching by existing holders of
sterling from British government securities to local authority deposits. See
Economic Trends, September 1965, p. v. The impact effect of such a switch on the
domestic banking system, however, would still be to increase liquidity.

inflow of funds after November 1964, was employed more cautiously after mid-1965, presumably to avoid a repetition of the inflow. This was partly because of objections to the policy raised by other countries in the OECD's Working Party 3.

Altogether, inflows of liquid funds have not been an important obstacle to U.K. monetary control by comparison with the impact of fiscal policy and the desire to cosset the gilt-edged market. What the inflows did, both in 1964 and in 1967 and also previously in 1960, was to conceal the underlying balance-of-payments position from the public and even to some extent from the authorities. This certainly made for bad policy, but it is a rather different point.

III.   The Impact of Monetary Policy

The most controversial aspect of recent monetary discussion is the link between money and expenditure. The fourfold impact of monetary policy sketched in Section I is widely accepted in qualitative terms. The trouble arises in quantifying. There are plenty of intelligent guesses—policymakers have to use them all the time—and there is a lot of econometric research, mostly in the United States. But this research has not produced any generally agreed estimates of just how quickly monetary policy acts or of how big its effect is when it does act. There is also a good deal of argument about whether it is sufficient to look at the quantity of money and its relation to national income, or whether a more detailed analysis of the financial structure is needed. The former is the view of the quantity theorists, headed by Milton Friedman in Chicago; the latter is typified by the Radcliffe Committee's concern over the 'general liquidity position' of the British economy.

Evidence produced by the quantity theorists tends to show that 'the economy has a stable demand function for money'. But this conclusion is not sufficient to guide policy. Friedman himself has long maintained that discretionary policy cannot stabilize the economy from year to year because of the long and erratic time-lags involved in its operation. Other monetary researchers have disputed his evidence and conclusions, and some recent work in the Federal Reserve Bank of St. Louis appeared to throw up a strong relationship in the post-war period between short-run changes in the U.S. money supply and in U.S. GNP. It turns out, however, that this relationship holds only for the 1960s and not at all for the

1950s. Moreover, the coefficients in the St. Louis regression equations are quite different from those found in a more complete model of the U.S. economy recently constructed by a joint team from the Federal Reserve Board in Washington and the Massachusetts Institute of Technology.[1]

The money supply and GNP are both substantially affected by public expenditure and the budget, while public expenditure is influenced little or not at all by monetary policy. So overall correlations of GNP with the money supply may not tell us much about the impact of monetary policy. In other words, whether to express the objectives of economic management in terms of a target for the stock of money is a much broader question that that of the impact of monetary as against fiscal measures on private consumption and investment.

In the United Kingdom the relative merits of monetary and fiscal instruments for controlling private outlay are difficult to analyse for two reasons. First, the two types of weapon have usually been applied in unison. Restrictive policy in particular has often involved a 'package deal' of fiscal and monetary measures combined. What can be said is that these package deals were invariably effective, though their timing and dosage were not always appropriate. In 1968, for example, neither fiscal nor monetary restraint was brought to bear quickly enough. But the more extravagant claims of the monetarists—notably that the increase in the quantity of money prevented tax measures from checking the rise in private consumption—were not borne out. Despite a decline in the personal savings ratio (from 7·9% in 1967 to 7·5% in 1968), real personal consumption rose less between the second halves of 1967 and 1968 (0·7%) than in the following twelve months (1·1%), when credit was much tighter.

Secondly, until the mid-1960s the UK monetary system was living out the after-effects of World War II and cheap money, namely high liquidity and a low starting level of interest rates in a period of unprecedented creeping inflation. The situation is now much more favourable to monetary policy, but it needed more than ten years to

[1] A very useful discussion of all this is Richard G. Davis, 'How much does money matter?', *Federal Reserve Bank of New York Monthly Review,* June 1969. The article by de Leeuw and Gramlich quoted earlier was reporting results obtained from the Fed.–M.I.T. model.

absorb the surplus liquidity and nearer twenty to raise interest rates
to a level which took reasonably full account of inflation and its
expected continuance.[1]

This process of adjustment can be looked at either in 'quantity
theory' or in 'liquidity' terms. A quantity theorist would say that
Britain began the 1950s with a ratio of money to income far above
the equilibrium level. He would therefore expect the ratio to decline
—the velocity of circulation to rise—in the succeeding years. This
is exactly what happened. The ratio of clearing-bank net deposits
plus currency in circulation to GNP fell from 50% in the early 1950s
to 35·6% in 1963 and 34·5% in 1967. In 1968 it rose to 35·7%.

Looking at the same process in 'liquidity' terms, one must examine
in more detail the changing balance-sheet positions of borrowers and
of credit institutions. Thus, the non-financial private sector has
become more dependent on outside finance. This applies particularly
to companies. Bain pointed out in his 1967 paper that the proportion
of companies' capital expenditure financed by borrowing and
changes in liquid assets rose from 19% in 1954–55 to 29% in
1964–65.[2] It seems to have remained at about this level in 1967–68,
though a large unidentified element in the statistics makes it difficult
to speak with confidence.[3] The expansion of business borrowing from
banks continued at a slightly slower pace after 1965, owing to the
ceilings on advances; but capital issues were over 20% higher in
1967–68 than in 1964–65. A striking feature of the monetary squeeze
during 1969 was the tightness of the capital market and the failure
of numerous company issues. This must have affected fixed investment in 1969–70.

In the personal sector the evidence is more ambiguous. It has long
been agreed that private housebuilding is affected by changes in the
cost and availability of mortgage finance; and also that the demand
for cars and other durable goods is influenced by changes in hire

---

[1] On this see the two articles by A. J. Merrett and Allen Sykes, 'Return on
equities and fixed interest securities', *District Bank Review*, December 1963 and
June 1966. Also M. J. Farrell, 'On the structure of the capital market', *Economic
Journal*, 1962.

[2] A. D. Bain loc. cit., p. 167. His source was 'Company Finance, 1952–65', *Bank
of England Quarterly Bulletin*, March 1967. 'Capital expenditure' is broadly
defined to include not only fixed investment and stockbuilding but also overseas
investment, purchase of U.K. company securities and changes in hire purchase
and other credit extended.

[3] *Bank of England Quarterly Bulletin*, June 1969, p. 150.

purchase terms. More recent investigations have detected a broader sensitivity of such demand to general credit conditions, with personal borrowing from banks playing a significant joint role with hire purchase.[1] However, individuals have also built up substantial holdings of liquid assets in the 1960s, especially deposits with building societies and trustee savings banks, which can be drawn down when credit is tight. Something of this sort seems to have happened in 1968, when restraint on personal borrowing and increases in indirect taxation were accompanied by a small decline in the personal savings ratio.

As regards the financial institutions themselves, both banks and others, such as insurance companies and pension funds, have gradually reduced the proportion of government debt in their portfolios. The clearing banks became 'loaned up' only in about 1964, the year when the share of advances in their total assets touched 50%. Since then, it has fluctuated mostly between 47 and 50%. The significance of this is supposed to be that financial institutions are now much less willing than formerly to accommodate private borrowers by switching from public to private debt within a given total portfolio. A quantity theorist would, of course, argue that this is the wrong way to look at it. If such asset switching is possible with a given quantity of money, it must be because the non-financial public has sufficient spare cash to take up the government debt, and what the whole process does is to raise the velocity of circulation. If, on the other hand, the government debt (or some of it) is bought by the authorities, then the effect is to increase the quantity of money. Either way, the problem is that there is too much cash around which the authorities are, evidently, unwilling to absorb.

It can be argued that the 'liquidity' or 'credit' approach is more illuminating in the case where the velocity of circulation rises, because the quantity theory does not explain how velocity is increased. But the 'credit' approach in turn neglects other cases. Suppose that bank loans to the private sector remain unchanged, but the authorities allow an increase in the quantity of money and the banks achieve this by buying government paper from the public. This is precisely equivalent to expanding bank advances, even though the ratio of public to private debt in the banks' portfolios has actually risen. The possibility is a perfectly realistic one.

[1] See 'Personal saving and financial investment, 1951–65', *Bank of England Quarterly Bulletin*, September 1966.

In March 1968, for example, the U.K. non-financial private sector, mostly individuals, was holding some £5,800m. of marketable government debt plus a further £3,900m. of non-marketable debt.[1]

With the U.K. authorities now professedly paying more attention to the quantity of money than in the past, interest in the subject seems bound to grow in academic circles in the next few years. The quantity theory also lends itself more readily to econometric analysis than the 'credit' approach.[2]

IV. Alternative Techniques of Control

Given the economy's high liquidity for much of the post-war period, and given the anxiety of the authorities not to upset the gilt-edged market through attempts to restrict the money supply, it is hardly surprising that monetary policy has involved a lot of improvisations and direct controls. The nature and effectiveness of these measures has varied considerably. Three main types may be distinguished:

(i) *Variable liquidity ratios for the banks.* Since 1960 the authorities have made use of the Special Deposits scheme, whereby the clearing and Scottish banks can be asked to place funds at the Bank of England, additional to their 8% cash ratio and not counting towards their minimum liquid assets ratio. The idea was to vary the amount of liquidity at the banks' disposal and so to discourage or encourage

---

[1] *Bank of England Quarterly Bulletin*, March 1969, p. 16. See also 'Does disinflation expand credit', *The Banker*, February 1962, for a discussion of financial policy in 1961, when something of this sort did happen.

[2] There is a statistical difficulty concerning the proper definition of 'money'. In Britain it arises from the number and importance of the non-clearing banks in the City of London—the accepting houses, British overseas bank, foreign banks and so on. This sector of the banking system grew very rapidly in the 1960s, and if its net deposit liabilities to U.K. residents are included in the money supply along with the net deposits of the clearing banks the ratio of money to income actually shows a rising tendency after 1963 (from about 39% to over 41% in 1968). It is, however, open to dispute whether deposits with the non-clearing banks are properly considered as money, or whether they are near-money, like deposits with hire purchase finance companies. Certainly the non-clearers, like other financial institutions, use the clearing banks for making payments, and do not have fixed reserves at the Bank of England. It is uncertain whether their operations involve a significant bank-credit multiplier. This depends on the extent to which their U.K. customers form a closed circuit in their banking operations. If the non-clearers are left out of the money supply the ratio of money to income from 1963 to 1968 was still falling slightly.

lending. In addition, the liquid assets ratio was itself lowered from 30 to 28% in a moment of monetary ease in 1963. The Special Deposits scheme has been more or less useless on its own, if only because the banks can manufacture their own liquid assets by lending on commercial bills and in other ways,[1] unless they are ordered not to.

An analogous but possibly more promising arrangement has recently been devised (though not yet used) for the non-clearing banks. Under this 'Cash Deposits Scheme' the Bank of England can ask these banks for Cash Deposits equal to a percentage of certain of their deposit liabilities in sterling.[2] In view of the highly competitive nature of the secondary banking system, this measure seems likely to have a definite effect on the non-clearing banks' earnings and hence on the cost and/or availability of their loans. The magnitude of the effect will, of course, depend on how the weapon is used; it will be limited to begin with by the fact that the initial Cash Deposits will carry interest at the Treasury bill rate, though the Bank of England reserves the right to pay less if the banks prove insufficiently responsive to official 'guidance' on the growth of their lending. The Bank has stated that the Cash Deposits scheme is not expected to eliminate the need for quantitative controls from time to time. This brings us to the second type of weapon:

(ii) *'Requests' to the banks* to limit their lending to the U.K. private sector both in general and for particular categories of business. The requests became more frequent, detailed and precise during the 1960s. Until 1965 they were directed to the clearing and Scottish banks only, but since then have been applied to all banks. Their effectiveness depends on the private sector being unable to sell government debt to the banks as a substitute for incurring debt of its own. A sufficient but not necessary condition for this is that the authorities hold the volume of bank deposits at the appropriate level, but this is subject to the difficulties mentioned earlier if the private sector actually attempts to sell government paper and

[1] See *inter alia* D. J. Coppock and N. J. Gibson, 'The Volume of Deposits and the Cash and Liquid Assets Ratios', *Manchester School*, 1963; and N. J. Gibson, 'Special Deposits as an Instrument of Monetary Policy', *ibid*, 1965.

[2] 'Control of Bank lending: the Cash Deposits Scheme', *Bank of England Quarterly Bulletin*, June 1968. An illuminating account of the secondary banking system, explaining why traditional notions of 'liquidity' scarcely apply to it, is J. R. S. Revell, *Changes in British Banking*, Hill, Samuel Occasional Paper, No. 3, 1968.

thus drives its price down. Usually, however, the imperfection of financial markets will prevent a good many borrowers from finding alternative finance, even if private sales of gilts could in principle force the authorities to increase the volume of money. It cannot be easy for small and even medium-sized companies to persuade individuals or fringe financial institutions to lend them significant sums at reasonable cost. The risks of such lending are considerable and, quite apart from the risk premium, heavy demand is bound to push up fringe interest rates to really high levels in a period of squeeze. Thus, direct controls on bank advances have probably had a significant effect. They do, however, create an incentive for new financial channels to spring up as a means of escaping the net, and in the long run the net may have to be cast progressively wider in order to keep trapping the same volume of fish.

(iii) The third type of control is *regulation of the non-bank financial intermediaries*, so far essentially the hire-purchase companies. It might be thought that this is precisely an example of 'casting the net more widely' in order to curb alternative sources of finance to bank lending; but this is not what happened historically. There was a lot of discussion some years ago about the possible destabilising impact of financial intermediaries. It was thought that they might be able to frustrate orthodox monetary restriction by attracting extra deposits and thus raising the velocity of circulation in direct response to a fall in the quantity of money. Little evidence was found, however, that this had actually happened. The post-war growth of non-bank credit institutions appeared rather as a steady trend, with no special tendency to accelerate in periods of squeeze.[1] For the United Kingdom this is not entirely conclusive, since hire purchase regulations have in fact been used as a policy weapon since the early 1950s. But, in any case, the argument for controlling financial intermediaries does not depend on their being destabilising. The controls are simply part of the general approach of credit rationing based on imperfect financial markets. Hire purchase regulations are a particularly valued weapon because they are known to have a pronounced effect on consumer buying (for the same reason

---

[1] See, for example, G. Clayton, 'British financial intermediaries in theory and practice', *Economic Journal*, 1962. Rather different evidence has been found on trade credit among commercial and industrial firms, which does seem to have been increased in periods of squeeze, allowing business to economise on cash balances. See R. G. Lipsey, and F. P. R. Brechling 'Trade credit and monetary policy', *Economic Journal*, 1963.

they are thoroughly disliked by producers of durable goods), and because they act essentially on the *demand* for credit by altering its price and so do not interfere with market forces to the same extent as quantitative ceilings on bank advances. Nevertheless, as already pointed out, they too may eventually get blunted if consumers go on accumulating liquid assets in order to draw them down when credit becomes tight.

V. Conclusion

The discussion may be summarised in the form of four main conclusions. First, as has often been said before, monetary policy in a mixed economy cannot be considered in isolation from fiscal policy. The public sector now purchases directly almost one-third of the U.K. gross national product and makes transfer payments to the private sector equal to a further 20%. Monetary restraint on private outlays must be supported by government control not merely over the balance of the budget but over the trend of public expenditure in relation to national resources.

Secondly, in stabilisation policy nothing succeeds like success. If the public come to regard sharp reversals of policy as the norm, and especially if severe periodic credit squeezes are expected, they may take precautionary measures, weakening the impact of policy over the long haul. There are already some signs of consumers doing this. If the present increased dependence of companies on external finance is over-exploited, they may react in the same way later, when policy is eased.

Thirdly, the variety of monetary weapons and controls that has been employed in the U.K. seems justified by circumstances. The size of the national debt creates problems for restrictive open-market operations, while the complexity of the financial structure means that direct interventions to alter the cost and availability of credit are best carried out at several different points. Monetary management, in a slower moving and less systematic way, has acquired something of the quality of tax law. Regulations are made, loopholes found in response, additional regulations made to cover the loopholes and so on.

Finally, whatever its shortcomings, the quantity theory of money offers a sounder basis for monetary policy than the alleged need to maintain an orderly market in government securities. If in periods of squeeze the public try to sell government debt, one cannot assume that their intention is to hold the proceeds in cash rather than to facilitate, directly or indirectly, expenditure on goods and services. It is to be hoped that there will be further experimentation with debt management techniques and a continuing effort to adapt them to the requirements of monetary control.

6

Pricing and Investment Policies of Nationalised Industries

Michael V. Posner*

Introduction[1]

How should nationalised industries conduct their financial affairs? It is generally agreed that, while profit maximisation may be, subject to all sorts of reservations, a socially desirable policy when practised by ordinary companies in a highly competitive situation, for various reasons it will not do for large public corporations, who either enjoy statutory monopolies or operate under conditions of highly imperfect competition or oligopoly. Similarly, the public service rule—'to produce such goods in such quantities as will best serve the public'—is too imprecise and unspecific in its recommendations. It has proved necessary for governments and the public corporations themselves to move forward to more specific rules affecting individual facets of their behaviour; academic economists have sometimes led, sometimes followed, and sometimes merely heckled at this process of rule formulation. This paper attempts to assess the present situation and to see how far present practice is reasonably consistent with economic analysis and commonsense.

Attention has been concentrated on three types of decision-making:—

(1) What quantity of investment funds should be spent by indi- individual corporations in a run of years, and in what physical

---

* Fellow and Director of Studies for Economics, Pembroke College, Cambridge.

[1] The arguments in this paper, and its mistakes, are entirely the responsibility of the author, and in no way represent the views of any Government Department with which he has been associated. British work on this topic has been much urged forward by Mr. J. L. Carr, Professor M. Peston, and Mr. R. Turvey, wearing their official, quasi-official and academic hats. (The results of their work may be seen, through a glass darkly, in, respectively, Cmnd 3437, the *Reports* of the House of Commons Select Committee on Nationalised Industries, and the *Reports* of the National Board for Prices and Incomes.) I hope they will not find too much error in this paper.

equipment ('techniques of production') should the funds be embodied?

(2) What should be the general level of prices charged by a public corporation and how should the price relativities of different products be set?

(3) At what level of surplus or deficit on operating account should the public corporation aim? (A more familiar and traditional way of putting this question is to ask about the degree of 'self-financing' of investment expenditure to which the corporations should aspire.)

These different facets of behaviour are not independent of each other, and we will see that, to some extent, when two of the three questions have been aswered an answer for the third can be implicitly deduced. Nevertheless, we will consider the three questions separately for ease of exposition.

The General Policy Framework

Before we discuss these rules for 'decentralised decision-making', we must note briefly that, for almost all the nationalised industries, a general framework of policy has had, in practice, to be laid down by the Government. Perhaps this is not a coincidence—industries may in fact become 'nationalised' just because the 'externalities', or divergencies between social and private costs, are so important in their case: this would be an appealing rationalisation of the political process of nationalisation! But, whatever the cause (political or more purely economic), 'fuel policy', 'transport policy' and so on have been decided upon outside the framework of rules that we are basically discussing in this paper.[1]

Fuel policy, for example, cannot start on 'free market' assumptions. Foreign exchange saving and other traditional autarchic arguments perhaps, on certain assumptions, can be neglected. But there remain the major issues of the run down of coal, of the rate of depletion of the natural gas fields, of policy towards inwards investment by oil companies, which are inescapably public responsibilities.

[1] One of the reasons why the steel industry appears so strange a member of the nationalised brotherhood is that, so far, it seems free of these general policy directives. Whether it should or can continue to escape is another matter.

These strategic decisions set the scene within which the partial decisions discussed in this paper find their validity.[1]

Investment and the Test Discount Rate

Rules for investment behaviour, for profit maximising companies in the private sector, have been much developed and popularised by many writers in recent years. Although discounted cash flow techniques should in principle have been familiar to academic economists from writings over thirty years ago, rapid progress in their application stemmed from business schools and financial consultants rather than the academic world in the fifties and sixties. It can be shown simply that a firm will maximise its profits if it chooses amongst a set of investment opportunities open to it in the following way: range all the projects in descending order of the internal rate of return which they might be expected to earn and choose all those projects which earn a return in excess of the marginal cost of capital funds to the firm concerned. (Alternatively and significantly different results can sometimes be obtained by arranging the projects in order of their present value, discounted at a common rate of interest representing the cost of capital, but this difference between very similar approaches need not detain us here.)

By analogy, if the 'cost of capital funds' can be similarly defined for the public sector, the rule could be readily adopted by public corporations as well: but three difficulties, in ascending order of importance, must be noted. First, in many instances the size of an investment programme and the equipment in which it is embodied, are determined by expected growth of demand, and very little choice remains—this was, perhaps, most typically true of investment in electricity during the fifties. If the demand for investment funds is so inelastic, capital rationing cannot be achieved by interest rate variations—nor indeed by any other elegant device—only crude administrative 'cuts' can do the job. But in general there are grounds for believing that some flexibility does exist, even for relatively small changes in interest rates,

The second complication involves the whole argument about how to choose this 'cost of finance' or 'cut-off rate of interest' for use in the public sector. Even if we assume that the aim of Government

[1] Cf. *Fuel Policy*, Cmnd 3438 of 1967.

policy is to ensure that choices made in the public sector are consistent with independently given choices in the private sector, the conceptual and calculating difficulties are formidable. The special jargon term which has been invented—the 'test rate of discount' (T.D.R.)—emphasizes that this is a rate to be used for investment decisions particularly, and has no necessary close connection with any other interest rates used or paid, for instance on public sector debt. It is difficult enough for a firm in the private sector to choose an appropriate cost of capital—this would depend on the firm's credit standing, the extent to which it is able to increase its borrowing in debentures, the size of its existing equity issue, its expectation of the way market interest rates will move, its fear of take-over, and doubtless many other factors. It seems right, therefore, to consider the evidence about the return firms actually look for on investment, rather than to try to calculate indirectly on their behalf what that return should optimally be! What we should be trying to estimate is not the observed *average* rate of return in the private sector, but rather the marginal expected return on a slice of investment which may be competitive with marginal investment expenditure by the public sector. Even when we have found such a rate, however, there will be more complications. An ordinary firm will rationally settle its discount rate after taking account both of expected investment grants and expected Corporation Tax during the lifetime of its investment— these must be netted out before we take over into the public sector the test rate used in the private sector. But different investment projects attract different investment grants, and different firms have different expectations and aims. Obviously, a heroic amount of estimation and adjustment has to be introduced in choosing a T.D.R. or in deciding to change the test rate from time to time. The rate has been 8%, and in August 1969 it was raised to 10%.

Thirdly, there is a conceptual difficulty on which economists are not agreed and on which there should be more public discussion. We have assumed that the private sector dog should wag the public sector tail (although since the amount of investment done by the public corporations totals about as much as the whole of private sector industrial investment, we might well say 'some dog, some tail'). More precisely, the argument is that mis-allocation will occur unless the marginal return on investment funds is identical wherever the money is spent. Now, insofar as investment expenditure is at all responsive to the test rate, the higher the test discount rate, the less will be the amount of investment, as public corporations choose either less capital-intensive techniques or a slower rate of growth of capacity. But the rate of investment for the future, particularly in the public sector, should, it is argued, reflect more the community's time preference than the blind forces of the market as judged by corporate planners in the private sector. Some would suggest that we should use a far lower discount rate—of the order of magnitude of 4%—with a consequentially far larger investment expenditure in the public sector. Others, amongst whom I fear I must now count myself, take a more restrictive view and argue that for the foreseeable future there will be an extreme shortage of resources, both for the economy generally and for the public sector especially. In the general case, consumers have shown that they aspire to a standard of living that increases at a real rate of 3 or 4% a year, and in their role as wage- and salary-earners have demonstrated over the years their determination to secure such a rise in living standards at whatever price in terms of inflation and balance of payments difficulties. Given the rate of growth in productive capacity (which has shown itself only sluggishly responsive to Governmental and managerial activity in recent years) and the need to earn modest surpluses on balance of payments, there are just not sufficient resources available for a large increase in investment: consumers vote for a high discount rate, implicitly, when they press their wage demands or resist vociferously, and at the ballot box, further imposts on their spending.

Similarly, the demands on the public purse for education, health and housing (barely responsive if at all to changes in the T.D.R.) seem likely to exhaust the resources made available to the public sector by the present level of taxation or by those increases in the burden of taxation which might be found politically tolerable during the seventies. If we wanted more investment in total, we could work with a low T.D.R. and, simultaneously, try by various fiscal means to ensure that the cut-off rate was lower in the private sector as well, so that correct inter-sectoral allocation was preserved. But if we have to settle for a restriction on investment, the public sector T.D.R. must be high enough to accord with the private sector cut-off rate. Regretfully, therefore, we have to work to the allocational rule that investment resources should not be used in the public sector if they are expected to yield a return lower than that which they would actually be invested in the private sector. Both capital stringency and this consideration lead to a 10% rate.

Pricing

A large amount of academic literature, going back over half a century, has argued that in some sense welfare will be maximised if all producers are prepared to sell a marginal addition to their present output at a price which will just enable them to meet the marginal addition to their costs. Traditionally, this marginal costing rule was discussed in the context of an existing stock of capital. Thus, for instance, if the electricity supply industry has a surplus of capacity over the next few years, marginal additions to electricity sales should be sought if the price charged is just sufficient to pay the fuel, transmission and associated user costs of the existing equipment. Numerous objections have been made to this proposed rule:—

(1) Unless the public corporation can discriminate between a new customer and an existing customer (to which there may be 'welfare' and political objections) marginal cost pricing might involve a fall in the price of *all* goods sold, and hence to large financial deficits. The financial deficits would need to be matched by higher taxes, to maintain the pressure of demand in the economy as a whole. And higher taxes on other goods would lead to distortions in resource allocation which could be as bad as the distortion caused by having prices set at higher-than-marginal cost in a nationalised industry. I come back to this point later.

(2) Marginal cost pricing by one bit of the economy may not be the optimal strategy if the same rules are not applied by competing firms in the private sector. For instance, if natural gas is sold at its marginal cost, while fuel oil is sold according to some other pricing rule, 'too much' or 'too little' resources may be drawn into the gas industry. Many attempts have been made to avoid this objection, but none of them, as I understand it, have avoided the basic analytical difficulties. Nevertheless, most of us working in this field have, for good reasons or bad, made the practical judgment that resource allocation would on the whole be more likely to improve if prices moved towards marginal costs than if prices diverged even further from marginal costs than at present. But this is a judgment subject to several important provisos yet to come, and needs to be debated more thoroughly.

(3) If the market is growing, through time, at a fast rate (no doubt associated with growth in real national product) the relevant margin for the calculation of costs is not a small increment in output from existing plant, but an addition to the stock of plants. This view can be arrived at in many ways, but its essence is the judgment that it is more important for us to get the relative growth in capacity right than to achieve the optimal utilisation of existing capacity. (According to one group of theorists the short run marginal cost will always in equilibrium be identical with the marginal total costs of a new addition to capacity. But in my view, while this may be true in certain special equilibrium conditions, it is not a very helpful, practical assumption.) The object of setting prices correctly is to ensure the correct allocation of resources between industries, and if that allocation is changing through time the important thing is to get the rates of change right.

The relevant question, therefore, becomes: 'Should prices charged correspond to a reasonable estimate of the cost in the future of meeting a sizeable increment to the existing level of demand by the installation of new capacity?' This question is formalised by defining 'the long run marginal costs' (L.R.M.C.) as, very roughly, the present discounted value of both the capital and running costs of a new unit of productive plant, and the pricing rule suggested is that the public corporations should set their prices equal to L.R.M.C. This has become a slogan, and indeed an article of faith, in much of Whitehall and Westminster, to the muted applause of academic observers.[1] Considerable irony has been expended on those administrators and

[1] The 'marginal cost rule' has in the last few years, under the influence of operational research and engineering science rather than through economic theory, become far more sophisticated. (See R. Turvey, 'Marginal cost', *Economic Journal*, June 1968, p. 282.) The sophistication has arisen in part with respect to technical progress, and in part to the optimal combination of different techniques of production (in electricity generation, gas storage, different modes of delivering a given quantum of fuel oil, etc.): these are genuine economic problems of major importance, but are not germane to the general issues discussed in this paper. Thus it would be perfectly feasible for the electricity Bulk Supply Tariff (for sales from the CEGB to the Area Boards) to be constructed on the very purest and up-to-date marginalist principles (in fact it falls rather short of this ideal), while the Area Boards' tariffs to the final consumer were 'trimmed' by the considerations advanced in the present paper. To this extent, 'productive efficiency' (e.g. the best combination of techniques of gas production and storage) may be separated from 'consumption efficiency' (the presentation of the correct tariff to the final consumer).

officials of public corporations who have attempted to retreat from
the apparent purity of this rule by stressing in a boring way the
difficulties and complexities of calculating L.R.M.C. or the need to
move slowly towards the state of paradise where the rule would be
fully and permanently obeyed. I suggest that much of the irony is
misdirected and that some of the administrative caution is justified.

But certain parts of this doctrine are, I think, universally accepted
and will be fairly rapidly introduced. In setting the relative prices of
different products (electricity at different times of day, telephone
charges for trunk calls of varying distances and times of day, relative
freight charges on railways, and so on) the marginal costing rule
accords very much with commonsense. When I build a house and
decide the form of heating to install, I do not then guesss the relative
price of oil, gas and electricity; guesses of this sort are extremely hard
to make and it may be wrong to be influenced too much by current
price levels. But in deciding whether to leave my electric water heater
on at night or in day-time, or in deciding to buy a storage heater
instead of a radiant electric fire, I should be influenced strongly by
the structure of tariffs offered to me by the area electricity board, and
this area electricity board in turn should be heavily influenced in
the tariffs it sets by the pattern of charges imposed on it by the electricity generating board. The sooner all these tariffs are set in ways
which adequately reflect different patterns of costs at different times
of day, the lower will be the cost of my electricity for a given level of
comfort and convenience and the lower will be the absorption of
resources into electricity generation and distribution.[1] This, an

[1] I fear that this argument is a retreat to the old and discredited notions that
allocative bacon could be saved by insisting that prices should at least be *proportional* to marginal costs, even if equality had to be resisted. (See R. Turvey's
essay in *Public Economics*, edited by J. Margolis and H. Guiffon (1969), pp.
336–343, and the discussion on pp. 547–550 of that volume; and P. M. Rees,
Economica, 1968, p. 260). But I would venture to be unrepentant. I can see no
distributive consequences of preferring, e.g. gas peak lopping through storage to
peak lopping through 'interruptible' final contracts: and the correct social choice
between those alternatives requires only that the proportionality rule between
'firm' and 'interruptible' selling contracts be maintained. Perhaps the most
fashionable current view of marginal cost pricing is embodied in the Ministry of
Power *Observations on North Sea Gas* (Cmnd 3996 of 1969): 'The Minister
concludes that there are good grounds for charging prices close to long-run
marginal costs to those consumer classes that tend to be relatively sensitive to
price, while setting other parts of the industry's tariffs above marginal costs in
order to make a contribution to the industry's overheads.' This doctrine of
discrimination *between customers* is not inconsistent with the doctrine, advanced
above, that the charge for peak and off-peak services should be determined
jointly by the costs of peak-lopping and the relative strength of consumer demand
at peak and off-peak times. Both are devices designed to obtain some of the advantages of marginalism while still allowing nationalised industries to limit their
demands on the Exchequer; both are compromises subject to attack from purists.

economist who is prepared to forget all sorts of consequential changes may say, is a good thing. (In practice there are many complexities in tariff-setting and we obviously need to compromise between unintelligible complexity and potential instability on the one hand, and insensitive over-simplification on the other.)

But L.R.M.C. pricing does not entirely evade the difficulties which old-fashioned short-run marginal cost pricing encountered. If a one-for-all improvement in technology occurs, the cost of producing from the new plant is below the cost of producing from the old ones. If one corporation owns all plants, and cannot discriminate in its pricing, the L.R.M.C. pricing involves 'losses' on the old plant, and the difficulties of point (1) above[1] reappear. It is true that if technical progress is expected to be continuous, this argument is mitigated and may even (under very special conditions) disappear, because the cheaper we expect tomorrow's plant to be the more it 'costs' us to invest in today's design, and hence the nearer is the 'marginal cost' of today's plant to the cost of existing, old-fashioned plant.[2] Despite this important point, to follow blindly the slogan of L.R.M.C. pricing can involve costs: either the costs of distortion from a higher level of taxation, or the costs of forgoing the benefits from a higher level of public expenditure. It is for this reason, I suggest, that the independent existence of 'financial targets' can be defended.

Financial Targets

The argument so far can be summarised as follows. At any point of time a public corporation is faced by objective demand conditions in the market in which it expects to sell. These demand conditions can yield, subject to great uncertainties of estimation, prospective markets for products at various alternative constellations of prices. Technical assessments can be made of the costs of meeting certain levels of demand, given that there is an implied requirement on the corporations actually to earn the test discount rate of 10% on new investment. The corporations will proceed to invest in the maximum amount of plant which would lead them to be able to sell the complete capacity output of that plant at a price equal to marginal cost,

[1] See p. 98.

[2] Cf. R. Turvey, *Optimal Pricing and Investment in Electricity Supply*, 1968, chapter 4.

including the cost of capital at 10%. Doubtless mistakes and errors would arise, and a process of iteration will be required. But the investment, pricing and cash flow positions of the public corporations would be in principle entirely determined. Nothing else needs to be assumed or laid down in order to produce a model which, subject always to risk, uncertainty and changes in the underlying technical or market conditions, is wholly determinate. Nevertheless, it is the practice of the Government to lay down in addition 'financial targets' for the industries, expressed sometimes in terms of rate of profit on book assets, sometimes as a number of millions of pounds of surplus on certain definitions. Several commentators have suggested[1] that financial targets either merely repeat what is already implied by the pricing and investment rules, or instead impose a requirement in contradiction to the other rules.

This argument has considerable force, but is open to three retorts:

(1) Pricing rules are difficult to define precisely, and there is often a considerable margin of error within which prices could settle and still be said to correspond to the slogan: 'Price equals L.R.M.C.'. Financial targets can be conceived of as fixing the surplus requirements of public corporations in a way which will determine where within the range of permissible price levels we eventually choose to settle.

(2) It is true that to charge prices materially above estimated L.R.M.C. involves some distortion in the allocation of resources. We have already seen, however, that the blessing given by economic theory to marginal cost pricing depends, in its strictest form on the assumption that the marginal cost rule is applied throughout the economy: we know this condition is not fulfilled in practice. We know, moreover, that Chancellors of the Exchequer often make harsh decisions on taxation which must lead inevitably to a certain amount of resource-misallocation. (In principle a uniform *ad valorem* tax on all goods would be a form of taxation that could avoid this particular difficulty, but the argument for and against such a tax would take us too far astray. We assume basically the present tax system.) It might be far better to allow the price of electricity or gas to be a little above its long-run marginal

---

[1] Cf. Select Committee on Nationalised Industries, Session 1967–8 (H.C. 371–I), *Report*, chapter V.

cost rather than to raise some other form of indirect taxation. This argument lets a particularly wicked looking cat out of the bag. Pricing policy by the public corporations must be seen in part as a form of indirect taxation by the Exchequer.

(3) More technically, it is by no means clear that a given T.D.R. uniquely defines the 'capital charge' which forms a component of the true marginal cost of producing a commodity. That the T.D.R. should be earnable on new investment is clear: the public corporation should not invest unless it believes that it *could in principle* charge a price embodying a 10% return on capital and still sell its goods. But this is quite different from saying that the price actually charged in a market should embody a 10% return not only on capital invested in the recent past, but also on the book value of existing capital assets. One way to crystallise thought on this problem is to ask—'What should be the natural consequences for national-ised industry pricing of the decision recently taken to raise forthwith the T.D.R. from 8 to 10%?' Reflection suggests[1] that it does not inevitably follow that prices themselves should forthwith be raised so that the new higher T.D.R. is immedi-ately earned on existing assets. It follows that, in the relation-ship between the T.D.R. and the optimal level of prices, there is a considerable amount of flexibility or 'give'. Once again, a role for financial targets is found as a way of choosing where, within a permissible range, prices should settle.

Risk and uncertainty

The above argument is conducted mainly on the assumption that the future is fairly well known, and that in particular developments in technical methods and market conditions can easily be predicted.

[1] Reflection proceeds as follows. If today, having just decided that the TDR is 'really' 10% rather than 8%, we are moved to sell electricity forward for 1980 delivery (*not* a silly contract, since power stations take five years to build and may not be scrapped for twenty-five years), then 10% should be the implied 'cost of capital' incorporated in the price. But for today's spot sales, the present balance between supply and demand may be a more relevant consideration. And for spot sales in 1980—well, our successors may have different views of the 'correct' TDR than we have—if only because circumstances will be different. Hence a decision to raise in the TDR at a point of time perhaps helps to create conditions *sufficient* to justify an eventual spot price increase, but does not in itself constitute the *necessary* conditions for such an action.

This is clearly not true. But there seems no systematic reason why one's views on pricing or investment behaviour should be fundamentally changed by taking account of uncertainty. Strategies for risk avoidance or risk reduction, and the choice of the degree of riskiness with which public funds should be used, have indeed to be made. It is usual to think about risk in the context of discussions of profit rates, and it is sometimes suggested that the T.D.R. should be increased to take account of the known riskiness of many public corporation operations. But even if it is true that the public sector as a whole should rationally be to some extent risk-averted (and it is difficult to make this argument stick), it is preferable to take account of risk by, for instance, considering a matrix of possible outcomes, rather than attempting to produce a single valued criteria of choice. In particular, it is not in general true that the more capital-intensive projects are the more risky projects, and hence it would seem inappropriate to take account of risk by raising the price of capital-intensive projects—that is, by raising the T.D.R.

Conclusions

There are three rules that have been developed for the running of public corporations:—

(i) An investment rule—projects should be undertaken only if the rate of return they are expected to earn is in excess of the 'test discount rate'.

(ii) A pricing rule—that prices should be equal to (or, less strictly, related to) 'long run marginal cost'.

(iii) Corporations are required to aim at certain 'financial targets', or levels of surpluses and deficits.

The investment rule is broadly applicable, but the main difficulty lies in defining a test discount rate. Comparability with what is done in the private sector is the aim, but it has been argued instead that the public sector should use a lower discount rate, to invest more for the future than private industry is inclined to. However, the paper suggests that there is such a shortage of resources, both in the economy generally and the public sector in particular, that a relatively high test discount rate must be used.

The slogan about 'long run marginal cost pricing' has been widely spread, but we should use it with discretion. It is roughly defined as the costs of production from a new plant of the latest design, and if a public corporation charge a price greater than, or less than, marginal cost then either too little or too much resources will be drawn into this line of business. This rule is probably most appropriate for deciding the pattern of relative prices (e.g. of electricity at peak and off-peak times) than in fixing the general level of electricity prices: this statement depends on a judgment (or guess) that secondary effects in other markets are less important when we are fixing the relative prices of similar products than when we consider the level of surpluses and deficits from the public sector as a whole. In any case, long run marginal cost is a far from simple concept, and depends (amongst other things) on necessarily uncertain guesses about the pace of technical progress in the future.

If we adhered strictly to an investment and a pricing rule, in conditions of certainty, stability and equilibrium, financial targets would be redundant; the level of surpluses or deficits from the public corporations would be determined, and 'targets' would have to be adjusted correspondingly. But, in the real world, there is sufficient 'give' or flexibility in the pricing and investment rules for financial targets to play an independent role. In deciding whether targets should be low or high, the authorities should be swayed by two related considerations:—

(i) Although distortion may arise from charging prices above marginal cost, distortion necessarily arises from any form of taxation designed to meet from the public purse the deficits of public corporations;

(ii) There may in any case be a need to raise net revenues from the public corporations to contribute to the general finance of public expenditure, or to stabilise the economy—to this extent the financial performance of the nationalised industries must be seen as part of general government fiscal policy.

7

The Management of Mergers Policy

Alister Sutherland*

Summary

Mergers alter market structure; and economists are concerned about market structure because of its impact on the performance of companies.

Tables on pp. 112 and 115 show the enormous increase in merger activity in recent years. It is argued in Section III (pp. 116 to 121) that this upsurge cannot be readily justified by appealing to the notion that British industry 'needs' to have bigger companies (or bigger plants) in order to enjoy economies of scale; for the biggest British companies *dominate* the non-U.S. scene; and British plants are certainly no smaller than those of their non-U.S. rivals.

Moreover, once companies and plants are reasonably big, there is no evidence that a further increase in size in general confers any benefit via lower production costs or better research and development. The benefit which is certainly given to dominant companies by economies in marketing or finance may well not produce any benefit to the consumer (Section IV, pp. 121 to 126).

The arguments for *not* worrying about the impact of the mergers boom in making markets less competitive and more subject to control by a dominant few thus look very feeble. I argue in Section V (p. 126 onwards) that the Board of Trade's procedure—eight references of mergers for investigation by the Monopolies Commission during a period when 120 mergers created or strengthened monopoly positions—would only make sense if there were overwhelming evidence that nearly all mergers involving companies already large improved performance (i.e. lowered costs or increased innovation) by more than they reduced competition. Since that assumption is not apparently justified, my conclusions for policy changes are:—

* Fellow and Lecturer in Economics, Trinity College, Cambridge.

1. The question in the Monopolies and Mergers Act 1965 should be amended so that the Board and the Commission have to ask whether a qualifying merger is likely to be positively in the public interest. (At the moment, even a reasoned conclusion that a merger is not against the public interest does *not* carry this implication.)

2. In qualifying mergers involving a company already in the top hundred—with capital employed of above £50m.—or where a merger would take a company into this size group—the onus of showing that there *are* likely to be net benefits to the public interest should be on the company. (At the moment there is terribly little quantification of effects; and no check that they are actually obtained.)

3. For the very biggest companies, say the top twenty-five, only the serious promise of really spectacular improvements in performance should be an acceptable justification. (If companies with capital employed of more than £200m. are not big enough already, then who is? And if they cannot add to their size sufficiently rapidly by *internal* growth, then who can?)

4. If working rules were to be published showing the kinds of mergers which would always be referred to the Commission (incorporating 2 and 3 above, for instance) that would reduce the pressure on officials and Ministers; would avoid apparent inconsistencies; and would give more assurance that, where the potential detriments are most serious, the improvements in performance are commensurate. Such 'guidelines' would *not* be like those used in the U.S.; there, a merger caught by the guidelines will almost certainly be *prevented* (unless it is modified, as in BP/Sohio, so as not to infringe them); here a decision always to *refer* the top hundred for investigation would still leave the issue open, so that the particular benefits and detriments could be examined.

I

The prejudiced might wonder what a paper on mergers policy is doing in September 1969 at a meeting concerned with economic management of the economy. Is it included merely as a terrible warning about what can happen if government does not in fact attempt to intervene, but leaves market forces too much to themselves? That is to overstate the degree of potential catastrophe that inefficient policy in any one field can produce but my main conclusion is certainly that the balance of current policy is inappropriate; and that pragmatic intervention in particular cases without more attention to a coherent general framework, and more access to resources for proper economic investigation, is bound to produce inefficient policy.

However, it may be useful to remind ourselves at the outset of the limitations of the subject matter. In discussing mergers we are mainly considering those increases in the absolute sizes of some companies which are brought about by acquisition rather than by internal or organic growth. That is an important piece of information about one facet of what economists call market structure—but it is perhaps worth pausing to remind ourselves of two things. First, there are other important structural features in addition to absolute size. For instance, the number of other sellers in the markets concerned, and the size distribution of their market shares. Thus economists distinguish at least between atomistic competition, tight and loose oligopoly, and single firm domination. Again, the number and size distribution of the buyers matters; if they are few and large we predict less freedom for even dominant sellers. Moreover, the likely behaviour of demand makes a difference; is the market expanding, and how fast? Again, the ease of entry into the market, and the ability to expand within it are vitally important. Here we mean not just the barrier to imports, by tariff or otherwise, but obstacles to the appearance of new firms, or to the diversification of existing ones into new markets. These barriers to entry may be the result, for example, of economies of scale, in production or elsewhere; product differentiation, which may mean that massive advertising is needed to make entry feasible; or patents. So in talking about mergers it follows that we are not covering even all the structural changes that might have an impact on behaviour and performance. We are leaving out in particular the birth of new companies and the death, where it happens without the decent burial of a take-over, of old ones; and the impact on absolute and relative sizes of the more rapid internal growth of some companies than of others.

Secondly, we should remember that economists are interested in structure not for its own sake but because we think that information about it helps us to make predictions about behaviour and performance. By the *behaviour* of a company we mean the way it conducts itself in relation to its suppliers and customers, that is, its methods of trading. Objectionable methods might then include 'unfairness', predatory or misleading action, formal agreements or informal arrangements, and such practices as exclusive dealing. By *performance* is meant the company's achievements in economic and technical efficiency (by which we mean getting the best out of available opportunities) and in progressiveness (that is, in expanding the range of opportunities). Dimensions here include cost minimisation; the linkage of price to cost; success in meeting demand, both seasonally and in the long run; and the record of the introduction of new products as well as new techniques.

However, economists admit that structure does not tell you everything. We realise that changes in behaviour and performance can happen without apparent changes in structure, let alone without changes in ownership. Thus there can be changes in the degree of informal joint action of nominally independent companies, ranging all the way from explicit or implicit collusion in tight oligopoly situations to harmless joint support for the recommendations, say, of little Neddies about methods of investment appraisal. There can also be changes in the internal structure and policy of existing companies for whatever reason, for instance internal revolution in the Board room, or more acutely competitive performance by rivals at home or abroad. Hence the predictions economists make, based on the links between structure, behaviour and performance, are very broad general statements of the form 'other things being equal, a large dominant firm in a protected, moderately growing market will tend to have higher prices, higher profits and to be more sluggish than one not so structurally secure; but many things internal or special to a company may not be equal, especially the quality and aspirations of management'. So features peculiar to the individual company must come in if predictions about that company are needed. (Incidentally, anyone who doubts whether a theory which yields such a watered-down sort of prediction as this can be of any use in practice may like to consider a sentence in the last general report of the National Board for Prices and Incomes (July 1969; para. 47): 'Experience (with prices charged to final consumers) confirms that as a general rule the greater the degree of competition the less the need for a reference to the Board.').

So even a complete appraisal of merger activity would not include *all* the types of changes which might lead to reorganisation of U.K. industry; and equally a measure of merger activity at best reveals one area for *potential* change in how businesses are run. Hence there can be radical change without merger; and there can be merger without radical change. I have taken time to underline this elementary point since I shall argue later that one main foundation of current Government policy seems to be the idea that in practice it would be highly dangerous, because of the threat to industrial efficiency, to slow down merger activity. That is, Government does regard the volume of merger activity as some sort of indicator of how much industrial structure and action are changing; and it also regards all (or at least 97%—see p. 126 below) of such change as desirable. I submit that there is room for doubt about both these assumptions.

In what follows, there is some account of the basic statistics describing what has been happening (Section II). Then some of the reasons sometimes given for thinking that we should be worried about recent experience are examined. Although the main counter-argument seems to rest on the idea that the scale of U.K. plants or companies is in some sense less adequate than in other countries, the evidence for that assumption looks very feeble (Section III). Moreover, the arguments about just how beneficial are the effects of scale on economic performance are also rather weak (Section IV). Finally, in Section V some criticisms of current policy are developed, and some suggestions are made for radical reform.

II

There are two main sets of figures for expenditure on acquisitions. The one providing the longest run is derived as part of the analysis of the accounts of quoted companies conducted by the Board of Trade, and published under the heading 'Income and Finance of Quoted Companies'. Data from that analysis are given in Column I in Table 2. Column IV gives expenditure on trade investments from the same source; these are 'investments not amounting to more than half of the equity share capital in companies with which the company is associated by way of business and as such may, for some purposes, be regarded as akin to investment in subsidiary companies'.[1] Column V gives total uses of capital funds (including I and IV) for purposes of comparison.

It needs to be pointed out that this series in Column I means exactly what it says; and so it does not include 'true' mergers. That

---

[1] *Board of Trade Journal*, 1 November 1963. A detailed analysis of trade investments in 1963 is given in *Economic Trends*, May 1966.

is, these figures are about what an existing company A spent on acquiring an existing company B. In a situation where A and B merge to form a *new* company C (which acquires the assets of both of them) the amount recorded here is zero. For some years the official figures list separately the amount of the combined assets of such new C companies, as shown here in Column III. But you might think that it is undesirable either to ignore mergers in the total figures entirely; or to add on these amounts for the combined assets of merged companies (the whole of the assets of A and B) to the amounts shown for acquisitions (where only the assets of either A or B would be recorded, not both.) What we want is an indicator of the rate at which assets are being transferred; and one which is not affected by irrelevant formal differences in the way the transfer actually takes place. So in the case of these true mergers we should presumably like to include the amount that would have been recorded if there had been an aquisition rather than a merger. Thus we need a convention. The convention which best combines ease of calculation with general conformity with experience would be to record mergers as if the larger company had acquired the smaller. That indeed is the convention adopted by the Monopolies Commission for one special analysis of large companies.[1]

However, the Board of Trade, in the second and more detailed series of quarterly figures which it has been publishing since 1968 in the *Board of Trade Journal*, does not adopt this convention. Instead it uses the two more misleading ones—and makes matters even worse by oscillating between them. Thus the *tables* in the *Board of Trade Journal* for 14 March 1969, pp. 752–3, record expenditure in 1968 as £2312·7m.; and a footnote explains that this expenditure includes mergers on the basis that C has acquired A and B, so that the whole of the assets of A and B go in. On the other hand, this total figure of £2313m. does not appear anywhere in the *text* of the article; instead we are invited there to compare the expenditure on pure acquisitions in 1968 (shown here in Column II at £1779 m.) with the figures for acquisitions from 1964 onwards also shown here in II.[2]

[1] Reprinted in *Mergers: a Guide to Board of Trade Practice* (HMSO, July 1969), p. 53.

[2] In the years for which both are given, Column II differs from Column I because yet another different concept is used. Thus in II we have 'expenditure during the year on acquiring subsidiaries'. In I we have II *less* proceeds of subsidiaries disposed of *plus* net expenditure on minority interests to get 'expenditure on acquiring subsidiaries'. (See *Economic Trends*, November 1965, and *Board of Trade Journal*, 15 November 1968, p. 1340.)

Table 2: *Acquisitions and Mergers of Quoted Companies*[1]

(£m.)

	I	II	III	IV	V
	Expenditure on acquiring subsidiaries[2]	Expenditure during year on acquiring subsidiaries[2]	Merged assets[3]	Trade investments	Total uses of capital funds
1949	47			9	723
1950	35			15	996
1951	32			15	1474
1952	36			13	630
1953	82			− 5	687
1954	114			10	1194
1955	97			21	1547
1956	119			25	1574
1957	128			31	1546
1958	121			35	1190
1959	277		55	68	1717
1960	338			76	2541
1960	328		85	76	2427
1961	374		311	81	2238
1962	306	336	⎱	145	1918
1963	307	329	⎰ 186	79	2217
1964	478			11	2922
1964	505	502		19	3078
1965	493	507		83	3328
1966	397	447		21	2767
1967		822[4]			
1968		1779[5]	534		
1969 (half year)		553	15		

[1] Quoted companies in manufacturing, distribution, construction, transport and certain other services. Companies whose main interests are in agriculture, shipping, insurance, banking, finance and property, and those operating wholly or mainly abroad, are not included. Companies with assets less than £½m., or income of £50,000 or less, are omitted from 1960. From 1960 to 1964 the analysis is of companies in the population in 1960. From 1964 the base is the population of companies in 1964. Before 1960 there is chain linkage between pairs of years.

[2] These concepts are explained on pp. 110-111 above.

[3] Early years are rough totals only, from *Economic Trends*, April 1963 and November 1965. For 1968 and 1969 see *Board of Trade Journal*, 14 March, 21 May and 3 September 1969.

[4] This expected final figure is given by the Monopolies Commission, reprinted at page 41 of *Mergers*.

[5] *Mergers* gives £1653m. £1,779m. is from the *Board of Trade Journal* for 14 March 1969.

Sources: *Economic Trends*; *Board of Trade Journal*; *Annual Abstract*.

Now even if there were zero true mergers in 1964–67 inclusive—and there appears to be no official study to confirm or refute this—given that there were mergers involving total assets of £535m. in 1968, a fair indication of the scale in the upsurge of merger activity will *not* be given by leaving out true mergers entirely from the 1968 total. Equally a fair indication of any diminution of merger activity will not be given if the first half of 1968 is now calculated to include total assets affected by mergers when 1968 is compared with the first half of 1969 (when merged assets, as it happened, totalled only £15m.) Yet that is exactly what last week's *Board of Trade Journal* (that for 3 September 1969) does:—'In the first half of this year, expenditure on acquisitions was only 56% of what it had been in the first half of 1968—£568m. against £1,017m. (In the first half of last year there were three large mergers totalling £465m. between them).'[1]

The bracketed statement was of course left out of most of the Press summaries. Moreover, we see the Board using one basis when measuring upswings in activity (from £781m. in 1967 to £1,779m. in 1968, as the *Board of Trade Journal* for 14 March 1969, p. 752, puts it) and another when measuring downswings (from £1,017m. in the first half of 1968—which uses a basis giving £2313m. for the whole of 1968, and *not* £1779m.—to £568m. in the first half of 1969, in the *Board of Trade Journal* for 3 September 1969, p. 621). If the Board could be persuaded to adopt only one basis, the convention suggested above, and to adjust the series as far back towards 1949 as seems fruitful, such pseudo ironing out of fluctuations, and the policy implications that would follow if the merger boom were thought erroneously to have greatly diminished, would be avoided.[2]

[1] £465m. appears to be a slip for £523m. The *Board of Trade Journal* for 14 March 1969, p. 753, puts the British Leyland (£455m.) and English Calico (£67·7m.) mergers both in the first half of 1968.
[2] Other adjustments that might be considered at the same time are the inclusion of acquisitions of U.K. companies by companies operating mainly abroad; the inclusion of some measure of 'the joining of divisions with other interests outside the company' so that 'for instance the merger of the computer interests of English Electric, ICT and Plessey, to form International Computers Ltd.' (*Board of Trade Journal*, 14 March 1969) *would* enter the total; the inclusion of all acquisitions by all quoted companies, irrespective of the date at which the company entered the population (see notes to the Table 2 given above); and standardisation on the concept of Column II not Column I (see above).
That the existing series for acquisitions should exclude these items, and use Column I rather than II, makes sense when it is seen as a minor part of an exercise designed mainly as an analysis of the Sources and Uses of Funds of the quoted company sector, viewed as a continuing whole. The exclusions make less sense if we are interested in measuring acquisitions and mergers as comprehensively as possible.

For 1968 the total expenditure, on the convention that in mergers the larger company acquires the smaller, would then be about £1,985m. using the last balance sheet valuations. Thus 1968 as a whole still stands out as a peak so far, but not quite so loftily as the crudely mixed figures suggested. Equally, the extent of the downturn is not so marked as the Board suggested. On the crudely corrected figures, expenditure in the first half of 1969 would be about £560m.; and that in the first half of 1968 would be, on a comparable convention, about £694m.—that is £1,017m. less the assets of B.M.H. Ltd. and English Sewing Cotton Ltd. Thus the Board's comparison would have said that the first half of 1969 was about 80% of the first half of 1968.[1] Moreover, it is more remarkable that activity is still running at an annual rate[2] two or three times that found in the early sixties than that it is down to about three-fifths of the 1968 peak; for while the peak is plainly pulled up by a handful of really super acquisitions that is not the explanation for 1969—so far.

Table 3 showing the number of companies taken over by the quoted companies defined as for Table 2, divided between quoted and non-quoted companies, and the average and total amounts, fills out the picture. (None of the 'true' mergers is included here.)[3]
The following features stand out:—

(a) The number of quoted companies taken over between 1954 and 1968 was 1,103, the annual numbers rising from around 55 in the late 1950s to 140 in 1968. (There are about 2,000 quoted companies in all in 1968.)

(b) The average size of quoted company taken over rose from £1·2m. in the late 1950s to £10·8m. in 1968. Note that companies of

[1] Simply leaving out the mergers entirely from both upswing and downswing would of course give £781m. for 1967, £1,779m. for 1968 and £553m. for the first half of 1969. Comparing the half years in the way the Board did would then give £494m. for the first half of 1968 (£1,017m. *minus* merged assets of £523m.) as against an increase to £553m. for the first half of 1969.

[2] When there is no expected seasonality, and when small alterations in the dates of a few large acquisitions would so greatly alter the quarterly figures, it is perhaps safer to compare crude annual rates than to use the Board's method of comparing 'equivalent' half years. That would mean £1,120m. in 1969 as against £1,985m. in 1968. Fortuitously, this puts 1969 at 56% of 1968—although the Board had no right to expect it!

[3] The figures for 1954 to 1963 are from *Economic Trends*, November 1965, and refer to 'total expenditure on subsidiaries acquired'. This is yet a third concept, differing from that used in Column II of Table 2 in that previous trade investment holdings made in earlier years are included.

Table 3: *Total and Average Expenditure on Quoted and Non-quoted Companies Acquired*

	Quoted companies Total			Non-quoted companies Total		
	Number acquired	*expendi-ture (£m.)*	*Average amount*	*Number acquired*	*expendi-ture (£m.)*	*Average amount (£m.)*
Annual average:						
1954–58	55	67·5	1·22	237	48·6	0·2
1959–61	81	200·6	2·48	561	137·1	0·24
1962	62	191·3	3·1	574	166·7	0·3
1963	77	157·4	2·1	808	174·5	0·2
1964	71	262	3·7	868	240	0·3
1965	75	347	4·6	920	160	0·2
1966	78	330	4·2	727	117	0·2
1967	84	630	7·5	577	151	0·3
1968	140	1,516	10·8	458	137	0·3
Total 1954–68	1,105	4,373	3·9	7,800	1,800	0·23

Sources: Up to 1963, *Economic Trends*, November 1965. Thereafter, *Mergers*, p. 50.

this size are about 370 in the *Times* list, with turnover of around £15–25m. and with around 2,000–7,000 employees.

(c) The average size of non-quoted company taken over rose only from £0·2m. to £0·3m. over the period; and, although there were many more such acquisitions, the total expenditure involved was only £1,800m. as compared with £4,373m. for quoted companies.

Further, if we look only at the *very* biggest manufacturing companies, the Monopolies Commission has recently calculated for us that the 28 biggest companies in 1961 owned 39% of the total net assets of large (that is, with assets greater than £½m.) U.K. manufacturing companies. By 1968 the (new) 28 biggest owned 50% of the total assets owned by the survivors of these large companies—or something like 40% of all assets in the manufacturing sector.[1]

Up to the end of 1968, the Board of Trade, under the procedure of the new Act of 1965, had looked at 318 qualifying mergers. (For

[1] In making this comparison the Commission, as noted above on page 111, adopted the convention that, where A and B merge, the transaction is included as if the larger had acquired the smaller. See *Mergers*, pp. 42 n. and 53 n.

further details see Section V below). Excluding newspapers, to date
10 mergers have been referred by the Board to the Commission. In
the last eighteen months alone 44 acquisitions of assets over £10m.
have *not* been referred for investigation by the Commission.

III

Given that we can all agree that there is room for structural change
in U.K. industry, what are the reasons for thinking that these dry
figures indicate that there is anything to worry about? Or that the
sort of official worrying that we have now may be inadequate?

It should be admitted at once that some of the arguments by
which we are urged to worry are bad ones. The complaints of the
slothful as they are awakened by brash newcomers should be ignored
—'ungentlemanly' behaviour is in many cases what we want more of.

Nor is there much cause for concern if there continues to be rapid
turnover in the population of the very smallest companies, for they
often have good personal reasons (tax; retirement) for wanting to be
taken over and can disappear without harm to the public interest.

Nor is take-over by a foreign company a cause of worry *per se*.
It is even inconsistent with general balance of payments policy to
argue against such take-overs; at a time when short-run considerations make us discourage outward direct investment, they should
make us want to encourage inward investment. Takeovers by foreign
companies may, however, indirectly indicate cause for concern. If a
U.K. company is worth more to a foreigner than to another U.K.
company that presumably is partly because the existing assets and
know-how can be used more advantageously under foreign management; and we should rightly be concerned if the foreigner has better
access to this scarce commodity.[1] The main serious worries seem to
me to be the following.

In the first place, there is no systematic check that the industries
and companies most in need of reorganisation are getting it. That is
the antithesis of planning; and its existence follows directly from the
way policy is handled. The Government initiatives in encouraging
mergers which are desirable but would not take place without the
I.R.C. are vastly outnumbered by those which the market wants to
happen and which escape public scrutiny. It is also indicated more

[1] See C. P. Kindleberger, *American Business Abroad*, Yale University Press, 1969,
p. 11, quoting Stephen H. Hymer.

indirectly by such scraps of evidence as that there is no general tendency in the largest mergers for the less profitable to be taken over by the more profitable—although of course profitability is not a perfect indicator for this purpose; and in any case other indicators, such as liquidity or sales prospects, might give a different picture. But if we look at the accounts of the companies involved in the twenty-nine readily identifiable mergers where the assets acquired in 1968 were over £10m. we find that in about half the cases the acquired company had a rate of return 10% or more *above* that of its acquirer; and in less than one-third of the cases was its return 10% or more below.[1] That might not surprise those who see that a company making a breakthrough is indeed more likely to be taken over than to be doing the taking over. Such a company would do very well by expanding its market share on the strength of its lower price or better product; but if it did that it would lower the profits of all its non-innovating rivals, both by increasing output in total, thus exerting further pressure on prices; and by forcing a lower profit margin on the now higher cost producers. One of them might find that it would be less expensive to buy out the present value of the future profits of the innovator (at a price which exceeded the valuations of those profits by both the innovator and the market)—but then to be in a position to control the speed at which its existing assets were made obsolete (because it could now hold back the growth of the industry's output)—than to face the losses forced on it by its failure to keep up technologically. It is especially likely that the PV of the future profits of the innovator will be less than the PV of the loss through lower profits for the laggard until it can get its costs down if the innovator is very much smaller than the other. In that case the loser has to face a lower price on a much larger volume of sales than the one the innovator will initially make his profits on. And the appropriate discount rate for the innovator may be very high because of the risks of not conforming with Big Brother's way of doing things.

Secondly the arguments about scale are surprisingly weak. I turn first in the rest of this Section to questions connected with the idea that scale is deficient in the U.K. Subsequently in Section IV the strength of the connection between scale and desirable performance is examined.

---

[1] This result for the largest mergers is identical with what Rose and Newbould found when they looked at 46 acquisitions over £½m. in March–May 1967; in 24 of their cases the acquired company was 10% or more above, and in 17 below. See *Moorgate and Wall Street Review*, Autumn 1967.

Are British productive units too small?

Concern that U.K. industry is handicapped by small size of plants or
companies, together with the idea that it can offset some of the past
failures by mergers now, is frequently found in policy statements.
For instance:—'Many of the production units in this country are
small by comparison with the most successful companies in international trade, whose operations are often based on a much larger
market.' (From the White Paper introducing the I.R.C., January
1966, para. 3.)

Again:—'. . . Many of our older industries are still too fragmented
with companies and factories which are too small by present-day
international standards. In such industries there is clearly a need for
restructuring and rationalisation. And even in newer industries
British companies are much smaller than their international competitors.' (Speech by the President of the Board of Trade, 28 February 1969, reprinted in *Mergers*, p. 58.)

There clearly are particular cases where we have insufficient size in
company or plant or industry (the latter may be important if external
economies are large)—although it would be helpful if these three
distinct facets were more uniformly distinguished. But a glance at the
facts, where there are any, suggests that there is so far no general case
for saying that either U.K. companies or U.K. plants are small
relative to their non-U.S. competitors (I shall come to the comparison
with the U.S. in a moment.)

(a) *U.K. companies relative to non-U.S. companies.* The composition by country of the 200 largest companies, ranked by sales,
outside the U.S. is given annually in *Fortune*. In the list given on
15 September 1968 there are 21 nationalised companies (5 of them in
the U.K.) which I have excluded from this comparison. The other
companies in the top 200 divide as follows:—

Table 4: *Distribution by Country of Largest Non-U.S.*
Companies (excluding nationalised undertakings)

	U.K.	Germany	France	Japan	Canada
top 50	11	13	4	10	0
51–100	14	4	7	7	4
101–150	11	4	2	12	5
151–200	13	4	5	14	2
top 200	49	25	18	43	11

So relative to our competitors outside the U.S., if size of company really was so important they should be worrying about us, and not the other way round.

(b) *U.K. plants relative to U.S. and non-U.S. plants.* Here there is no new data to present. Professor Bain's study[1] analyses data from the mid-1950s for the average number of employees in the largest 20 plants for a sample of up to 34 industries in different countries. Taking employment for the U.S. as 100, Bain found indices of plant sizes in the U.K. running between 24 and 131, with a value of 78 for the median U.K. industry. But although the average U.K. plant, on this definition, was smaller than the U.S., for Canada the median was 28, for France 39, for Japan 34, for Italy 29, for India 26 and for Sweden 13.[2]

(c) *U.K. companies relative to U.S. companies.* We read in the Annual Report of the I.R.C. (June 1969, p. 7):—'We are an open trading economy. It needs to be remembered, for example, that *G.E.C.–English Electric* has sales well below those of General Electric of America and is only now of comparable size to other international electrical companies such as Philips NV or Siemens of Germany.' This kind of argument has some oddities. First, since the U.K. company is still only about one-third of the size of G.E., does this mean that it still is not big enough? If so, is the policy conclusion that we should shift resources into electrical engineering until it is big enough? Or should we shift entirely out of electrical engineering since it is doubtful whether we ever can be big enough? Moreover, would we not find that nearly all U.K. companies in all industries were 'too small' on this criterion—so that we could not rescue even one in each industry, even if we were prepared to face the consequences of having one-company industries. So if size of company is really so vital the correct conclusion seems to be that countries smaller than the U.S. have to decide *which* industries to have big companies in;

[1] J. S. Bain, *International Differences in Industrial Structure*, Yale University Press, 1966, p. 39.

[2] Unfortunately, Germany could not be included in Bain's study. G. F. Ray, in the National Institute *Economic Review*, November 1966, reports that in 1958 the average number of employees in all manufacturing plants was 84 in Britain and 76 in West Germany. Looking only at the very largest plants, those employing 1,000 or more, the average size of plant in Germany (in 1961) was 10% more than in the U.K. (in 1958). But there were 1,206 such plants in the U.K. as against 1,045 in Germany; and the German advantage in net output per head (in 1954) was much *greater* in this size class than in the smaller size classes.

and they should do it on the basis of where their own comparative advantage lies, not where the U.S. has its biggest companies.

Secondly, is size really so vital? Are there no efficient electrical companies in other countries smaller than this mystically appropriate size of G.E. (or of Philips—or of Siemens)? The answer is of course yes. The two biggest Japanese companies are smaller than either Philips or Siemens (with the second Japanese company only about half the size of Siemens); and, smaller still, Brown, Boveri in Switzerland is 'only' one-third of the size of Philips—and barely bigger than the former A.E.I.: and much smaller than the old English Electric. How do these companies manage to compete? Even closer to home, there are twenty-seven sizable subsidiaries of U.S. firms operating in the electrical engineering industry in the U.K. These averaged 1·4 times the 109 U.K. firms in profitability, and the biggest of them has capital employed of £64m.[1]—that it, it is about one-tenth the size of the G.E.C.–A.E.I.–E.E. combination. Explanations for the varying size of companies in the 'same' industry doubtless lie in the fact that, behind the facade of similarity, specialisation by product and by area occurs. But the point is that company size, by itself, explains very little.

Thirdly, is the market situation of G.E. fully characterised by saying that the company is three times the biggest U.K. company? The answer is no, because G.E. faces competition in its home market from at least three U.S. companies each bigger than the new U.K. giant; and it is perhaps worth remembering that the resulting competitive pressures were strong enough for some G.E. executives to find themselves in gaol not so long ago for seeking to escape them by colluding with competitors on prices, and so falling foul of the anti-trust laws. The U.K. company will not be exposed to this kind of competition from domestic sources. Moreover, when last calculated, the effective protection—that is the protection afforded to domestic value added by the nominal tariff rate—against imports of electrical machinery was as high as 30%.[2] We may be an open trading economy but we are far from fully open.

In short, this vague kind of international comparison tells us nothing, because neither size relative to some other company, nor

[1] J. H. Dunning, *The Role of American Investment in the British Economy*, P.E.P. Broadsheet 507, February 1969, pp. 132 and 177.

[2] B. Balassa, 'Tariff protection in industrial countries; an evaluation', *Journal of Political Economy*, December 1965.

absolute size, are either necessary or sufficient for the optimal use of resources, or for the ability to compete. It is for this reason that U.K. policy is supposed to rest on the pragmatic basis that each case of substantial increase in size brought about by merger must be looked at on its own merits. But if that is the policy, it should be seen to be carried out. In this particular case the Monopolies Commission was not asked to report, because the merger was under the auspices of the I.R.C. And the I.R.C. statement dealing with G.E.C., on pp. 32–36 of its annual report, gives no clue to the actual action to be taken by the merged companies; no quantification of its effects; and no quantification of the effects of alternatives, such as the hiving-off of the main product lines as separate enterprises.

The argument that the U.K. is in fact deficient in scale is therefore weak, on the present evidence. In any event, how strong is the connection between scale and desirable performance?

IV

One of the major reasons frequently given for dissatisfaction with excessive competition and the resulting fragmentation of markets is that either companies or plants will be 'too small'; that is, their unit costs of production will be higher than they might be if each of them had a larger market share and longer production runs. It is therefore not surprising that companies already large, or about to become larger through mergers, with large market shares will claim that, as a result, they have reaped economies of scale and also that these economies would be a serious loss if their market share or their security were diminished. The interesting questions are therefore two: Will a 'larger' company have lower costs than a 'smaller' company? The answer must not be assumed to be yes, especially when both companies are already large in absolute terms, and have large plants. Secondly, will the benefit of the cost reduction be great enough to offset the potential losses to the public that will flow from competition being less effective? The losses are relatively hard to quantify— for instance, will prices be raised further above the now lower costs, and, if so, is the net effect of lower costs but higher profits going to produce a price increase? Again, will obsolescent plant be scrapped as quickly as socially desirable? But some of the benefits, especially at the plant level, ought to be much more readily quantifiable. If they do not turn out to be large that might make it easier to decide which way the judgment should go.

What then is the evidence for scale economies?

(a) *Production economies.* J. Johnston's survey[1] of the U.S. and U.K. econometric literature on how average cost varies with plant size, as measured by output, shows that the almost universal tendency is for the average cost curve to be L-shaped; that is, unit costs do diminish with scale initially; but at quite low levels of output they level off; and thereafter increased output is not associated with lower average cost.

J. S. Bain analysed, admittedly in the mid-50s, twenty American industries in great detail.[2] He sought to establish the optimal scale of plant by searching the engineering literature for the scale of plant associated with minimum average cost. He found only one industry where optimal scale was more than 15% of industry capacity; and the median was $2\frac{1}{2}\%$. That is, there was 'room' for forty optimally sized plants in the average of his twenty industries. Bain then compared the average market share of the largest four companies in each industry with the estimated optimal plant size for that industry. The range was from unity for one industry (typewriters)—where the size of the average market share of the biggest companies *could* be explained by the need to have big plants—to 24·3 for flour milling; the median was around ten. That is, on average the degree of domination in the market, in so far as that is indicated by large market share, could *not* be explained by the 'need' to have big plants.

Bain found that that conclusion held when he checked for multi-plant economies as well. He found that the major reason for the persistence of companies so far in excess of optimal plant size was product differentiation and the barrier to the entry of new companies that this investment in the moulding of consumer preferences created.

Is there more local and more recent evidence?

It is noticeable that many of the companies recently acquired in the U.K. seem likely to be as large as seems to be necessary to secure production economies (see page 114, at (b), above). If new management can without radical physical reconstruction of the assets but simply by better organisation or distribution use the same resources to produce a better product at a lower price, then important questions seem to arise. Why did the previous management not use the

[1] J. Johnston, *Statistical Cost Analysis*, New York, 1960.

[2] J. S. Bain, *Barriers to New Competition*, Cambridge, Mass., 1956.

resources efficiently? Why was there not enough competitive pressure earlier to make them do so? Will there be enough pressure in future to maintain the new momentum? What is to be done in future if the new bigger giant shows signs of seizing up again—are we to have him merged into a yet bigger one?

There is little sign (and no official analysis) that the largest horizontal mergers (where the possibilities for production economies are presumably greatest) happen either when there is a technological breakthrough, or when demand suddenly accelerates. They seem to be much more frequent in industries faced with problems of decelerating or diminishing demand; and with a wide dispersion of competence either in economical production or in marketing. Similarly, it is hard to see a technical reason for the recent multiplication of such mergers over so wide a field of industries; have the opportunities been accumulating uniformly for so long; and what has suddenly induced the general rush to take advantage of them? The impression is left that many of these mergers are not concerned with grasping new economies of scale; but rather with easing the pain of exit of lagging firms. The danger is that the anaesthetic is being supplied too liberally.

I have recently analysed some Monopolies Commission reports, both on large firms and on mergers.[1] The Commission is not good at quantifying economies of scale, even where the company has been big enough for long enough for them to have been fully exploited. But quantification can sometimes be attempted from the evidence given in the Reports; for the large firms examined since 1965 the economies are *not* great.[2] For mergers, the evidence is that the economies, where they are quantified at all, are strikingly small, even as promises.[3]

The Economic Council of Canada has recently reported[4] the results of a questionnaire inquiry addressed to manufacturing companies which had made acquisitions during 1946–61. 46% reported that there had been negligible or no economies; 27% reported

[1] *The Monopolies Commission in Action*, Cambridge University Press, September 1969.

[2] Op. cit., pp. 16–17; 49–51.

[3] Op. cit., pp. 65–66. For the Commission's similar views on two later mergers see Unilever/Allied Breweries at p. 28; and Rank/De la Rue at para. 105.

[4] *Interim Report on Competition Policy*, The Queen's Printer, Ottawa, 1969, pp. 210–218.

economies in administration and management; only 10% reported
economies from integration of plants and use of raw materials.
(For the horizontal mergers only, the results were 35%, 33% and
15% respectively.) The data are not perfect, as the Council empha-
sises, but the absence of any claimed economies in so many cases, and
the non-importance of production economies, are notable.

A recent U.S. study[1] also concludes that production economies
are the hardest to realise after a merger, and often do not arise. In
short, the hoped for 'synergy' effect only happens when in fact some-
one works harder. That is $2+2=5$ only if there is a hidden input—
probably of $1\frac{1}{2}$—in managerial drive.

But even if the evidence for the realisation of production economies with scale is so weak, are there other areas where scale gives
economies?

(b) *Scale and research and development.* That the 'biggest' firms
do more is not claimed, or given much space, in Monopolies Commission reports. The argument that 'big' firms are sufficient if any
R. and D. is to be done is undermined by the observation that about
60% of U.K. R. and D. is concentrated in three industries—and the
same is not the case for the distribution of large firms.

The much more systematic U.S. evidence is against the view that
firms need to be enormous to do enough R. and D.—although it is
in favour of the view that firms need to be above minimal size.[2]

(c) *Marketing economies.* Here the question is not so much whether
bigness confers advantages as whether the public benefit is as large
as the private benefit. The argument of the duopolists in the Monopolies Commission's report on Detergents (pp. 33 and 94) is that if
there were more large companies, unit marketing costs would rise,
because now each of the companies would have to conduct selling
campaigns etc. involving the same kind of total expenditure as the
two existing major producers, while total sales volume would not
increase much. The consumer is therefore supposed to face higher
prices. The tacit assumption is that although there would now be
more competitors each of them would behave in the same way as the

[1] Kitching, *Harvard Business Review*, November–December 1967.

[2] See the survey by R. R. Nelson, M. J. Peck and E. D. Kalachek, *Technology,
Economic Growth and Public Policy*, Washington DC, 1967. Companies employing more than 5,000 were found to support inventive and innovative activity less
intensively relative to their size than companies in the 1,000 to 5,000 range.
See also F. M. Scherer, *American Economic Review*, December 1965, and June
1967.

duopolists did. It is more likely that the arrival of more competitors would lead to a change of approach, with the consumer being offered a lower price by some companies—which they could afford to do, because they had lower profits and because they had also reduced their unit marketing expenditure well below the old norm of 25% of the retail price. Hence the 'saving' in marketing costs, which is said to follow because the number of companies each spending on a lavish scale is being held down to two, is an illusion resulting from an incomplete analysis. This kind of behaviour will not continue if the structure becomes more competitive. Moreover, in this particular case, the high unit marketing costs are *not* necessary in order to expand demand sufficiently to allow low unit manufacturing costs; for there is evidence that economies of scale in production are not significant (see *The Monopolies Commission in Action*, pp. 49–51). Hence, in a more competitive market, with more and smaller companies, unit production costs would be no higher, despite the lower unit marketing costs.

Thus in all such cases we need to know whether the kind of marketing expenditure which dominant companies choose would remain the same if they were less dominant; whether high unit marketing costs are necessary to achieve low unit production costs; and, if so, whether the net result, allowing for a higher unit profit, is a lower price to the consumer. If these conditions are not all satisfied, we should regard the 'economies of scale in marketing' which are said to follow from the fewness of competitors as indicating that there is a high barrier to entry (as the Commission observes); and not that the rest of us are benefiting from anything.

(d) *Economies in finance.* The argument here is that it is easier and cheaper for the larger firm to borrow because risk is lower. But for this private benefit to be a public one we have again to show that there are economies of scale in production, or elsewhere. Otherwise the increased ease with which the larger company acquires or retains control over resources is no benefit. That is, we must distinguish 'larger companies make fewer mistakes' from 'larger companies are better protected against the results of any one mistake'. The former would be a public benefit of size; but the latter is mainly a private benefit.

(e) *Conclusion.* The topic deserves more systematic inquiry than this, but it is reasonably clear, I think, that there is no general tendency for enormous scale, as opposed to large scale, to be either necessary or sufficient for beneficial economies to be realised. Seen against this background, is anything wrong with current policy towards the increase in size by merger?

V

The Monopolies and Mergers Act, 1965, gave the Monopolies Commission important new powers. Since 1948 it had been possible for the Board of Trade to refer to it for investigation and report a monopoly in the supply of goods; that is, a situation in which one company produced at least one-third of the goods. Now the Board could also refer prospective or actual mergers, provided either that the resulting company would have a monopoly or that the assets acquired were worth £5m. or more; could hold up a merger until the Commission had reported; could then forbid or unscramble a merger; and could impose conditions in cases where the Commission found that a merger would be against the public interest without them.

The way in which these new powers have been used since 1965, and detailed guidance about the Board's current practice, have been recently amplified in the official handbook issued by the Board, *Mergers*. We are informed there that up to the end of 1968 the Board has considered 318 qualifying mergers, excluding 23 newspaper mergers (for which the Act prescribes a special procedure) and 24 banking and building society mergers. (Para. 81. The grand total to June 1969 was 430 (para. 78).) The Board was able to decide quickly whether or not to make a reference to the Commission: '90% of these mergers have been dealt with by the Board within three weeks and 75% within two weeks of their announcement or notification' (para. 60). Excluding newspapers, only eight mergers were then actually referred for fuller investigation by the Commission (and two more in 1969); and the Commission ruled against three of the eight (and against four of the ten).[1] The 318 mergers so expeditiously handled included 120 which qualified because they were horizontal mergers which enhanced or created a monopoly position; and 42 of these also qualified because the assets acquired exceeded £5m.

[1] Paras. 83 and 84. In the Barclays/Lloyds/Martins banking case the majority against was insufficient for a formal recommendation by the Commission. Formal recommendations were made against Ross/Associated Fisheries; United Drapery Stores/Montague Burton; and Rank/De la Rue.

1. To be happy that there should be only eight references to the Commission over a period when 120 monopoly positions were created or strengthened by acquisitions surely requires us to have too much faith in the effectiveness of the Board's internal vetting system. For where we are able to read the results of a 'full scale investigation by the Commission' taking up to six months (para. 25) we will still look in vain for answers to many of the kinds of questions which the Board says it regards as relevant, and can answer in two or three weeks, when taking the vital decision about whether or not to make a reference in the first place.[1] Thus the first criticism to be made of current policy is that it does not come near to guaranteeing that the decisions whether to refer or not are made in the light of sufficient information. For instance, we are told that in a non-contested merger the companies come together to the Board to state their case. We are not told how it is possible in that situation to probe carefully to see whether either party is making claims which the other regards as excessive; or whether some alternative merger would be even better. Nor is it clear where informed evidence of potential detriment will come from in such cases. Supposing that Rank/De la Rue had been an agreed merger, can we be sure that the information on some of these matters contained in the Commission's report would have been available to the Board? Moreover, the Commission itself has recently complained that not enough information is available to it, even of a basic financial kind, and has presented the Board with a long list of changes which it regards as desirable in the presentation of company accounts. (See *Mergers*, pp. 48 and 54). If even basic financial information is lacking—such as the breakdown of company sales figures by main type of product—how can the Board hope to answer properly such more fundamental economic questions as whether costs are as low as they could be? If legislation is necessary to make sure information is forthcoming, that nettle should be grasped.

2. The President says that he will rely more on 'assurance as to future behaviour' in doubtful cases where, without them, he might have made a reference to the Commission.[2] One does not have to be

[1] See, for instance, pp. 8 to 14 of the handbook for the many difficult issues which are considered by the Board in the case of horizontal mergers. For a fuller critique of the Commission's reports on mergers up to mid-1968 see *The Monopolies Commission in Action*, Part II.

[2] *Board of Trade Journal*, 6 August 1969, reporting his statement introducing *Mergers*. Para. 86 in the booklet lists eight very large mergers where assurances (not quoted) have been given.

an ardent believer in the original sin of businessmen—or to be unfairly surprised by such recent events as the non-realisation of promised productivity agreements—or the failure of television programmes to correspond very closely with prospectus—to regard reliance on undertakings as a very doubtful safeguard of the public interest. This is partly because the undertakings may easily be so vague that breaches of them would be undetectable;[1] and partly because after the merger has gone through there is no effective sanction even if a breach is recognised, unless a government, previously reluctant even to refer a merger, would now be prepared to contemplate the much more difficult task of breaking up a completed merger. The necessity to ask for undertakings about behaviour surely reveals that the merger would make the market insufficiently competitive. Before acquiescing in such a development, the Government should require that there should be evidence of performance benefits large enough to convince the Commission that the structural detriment would be greatly outweighed.

If that strikes you as the type of question that needs to be asked, you will be perturbed by my next point; for that is that without a change in the Act the Commission will continue not to ask it.

3. The Board, in deciding whether it should refer, looks first for evidence of potential detriment. If preliminary enquiries reveal that possibility, the Board considers 'whether there appear to be such substantial offsetting advantages as to make it virtually certain that they outweigh the detriments' (para. 25). If not, the Board makes the reference.

This outline of the Board's procedure generates the expectation that the Commission will concentrate on spotting and quantifying the advantages of a merger; and that if benefits are not found to be really substantial, the merger will be rejected—unless of course the detriments which looked obvious to the Board turn out not to exist. However, this is not at all what happens. The Commission looks closely at the 1965 Act and sees that its task is to discover whether a merger would be against the public interest. It construes that to mean that it should pay most attention to the existence and size of detriments. Only if these appear to be very considerable will it look at all closely at the benefits.[2] However, the Commission does not require

[1] See my comments on this aspect of the BICC/Pyrotenax merger in *The Monopolies Commission in Action*, p. 60.

[2] Even then, when quantified at all, the benefits have so far been found to be remarkably small. See *The Monopolies Commission in Action*, pp. 65–66.

that the benefit should outweigh, that is be greater than, the detriment—it is enough if it equals it. Thus the Commission says repeatedly that it is looking to see if the merger is *against* the public interest, not whether it is actively *in* the public interest. Hence a favourable report quite clearly does not imply that the Commission thinks that the merger will be a good thing.[1] The logic of the Board's procedure in the referred cases, as now revealed in the handbook, thus seems to require that the relevant question is whether these mergers where the detriment is obvious are nevertheless, because of the benefits, actively in the public interest. The Commission does not interpret the Act in a way which would require it to answer that question. One conclusion therefore is that the Act should be altered to pose that question so that the cases about which the Board feels sufficiently doubtful to make a reference are explored meaningfully.

4. A more far-reaching conclusion, based on what is said in my earlier Sections III and IV above about the general arguments about the presence and effects of scale, as well as on the Commission's reports, is that the vetting procedure should contain some rules designed to make sure that many more of the borderline cases are put out for examination by the Commission. That would involve strengthening the Commission, and in particular its supporting technical staff. There is a strong case for doing that in any event, in order to improve the analysis and quantification in the monopoly references.[2]

More fundamentally, it would involve establishing and publishing some guidelines. The President has recently repeated his opposition to this kind of proposal[3] for reasons which he set out more fully in his February speech in Manchester.[4] In brief the President argued that the U.K., unlike the U.S., should remain pragmatic, deciding each individual case on its merits; and that it was too difficult to draft

---

[1] '. . . we have to decide not whether the merger is in GKN's interest or even whether it is positively in the public interest but only whether it may be expected to operate against the public interest.' Thus the Commission, in para. 126 of the report on the GKN/Birfield merger (Cmnd 3186, January 1967). For the attitude in the other references up to mid-1968 see *The Monopolies Commission in Action*, p. 68. See subsequently the report on Unilever/Allied Breweries (HC 297, 9 June 1969), para. 124. This proposed merger was subsequently abandoned by the parties.

[2] See *The Monopolies Commission in Action*, pp. 76–77.

[3] *Board of Trade Journal*, 6 August 1969, p. 346.

[4] Reprinted in *Mergers*, p. 60.

guidelines which would be both useful and yet flexible enough to avoid stopping desirable mergers.

It would certainly be a major policy change if we were to adopt completely the U.S. approach in these matters. But we need to distinguish much more clearly than Mr. Crosland did between the guidelines which might be set out here to enable the Board to decide when to *refer* a merger for fuller investigation; and the guidelines which are now used in the U.S. by the Department of Justice in deciding whether to start proceedings which will, given the U.S. statutes and case law, always almost *stop* certain kinds of merger. Saying that you will always refer a merger for investigation in given circumstances does not at all imply that the Commission's decision on the merits will always go one way, so 'the pragmatic and empirical approach' is not endangered. In short, the guidelines in the U.K. would perform a quite different function.

Deciding in detail just what should be in the guidelines raises a further question; and the U.S. numbers may not be appropriate.[1] But a start could be made. For instance, if my suggestions below (see p. 132) for shifting the onus of proof in some cases are not acceptable, the milder step could still be taken of saying that in the cases defined there a reference would always be made. The introduction of publicly known guidelines would be one obvious way of making sure that more of the doubtful mergers are given a proper examination.

The need to decide what the content of the guidelines should actually be in the U.K. allows a more fundamental issue to be raised.

5. The present procedure is geared to giving the benefit of the doubt to the merging companies. This would make sense if the

---

[1] It should be noted that the President's rejection of the American arithmetic rests partly on a serious misconception. As he reports, for instance, in a highly concentrated market—one where between them the four largest firms have 75 % of the market—the acquisition by one firm which already has 15 % of the market of a firm with as little as 1 % will be challenged. Mr. Crosland continues:—'Now in a huge economy like the United States, where large size is easily attained without loss of competition, this sort of arithmetic is acceptable. But in a smaller economy like ours, where necessary size may inevitably mean a certain degree of monopoly, such an approach could be very damaging in relation to international competition' (*Mergers*, p. 60). But this is to ignore the point that the relevant market is not necessarily, or even usually, coterminous with the whole of the U.S. economy. Instead it is restricted to the section of the country, or the line of commerce 'in which each of the firms whose sales are included enjoys some advantage in competing with those firms whose sales are not included' (Department of Justice, *Merger Guidelines*, May 30, 1968). For instance, in the BP/Sohio case 'the market' in question is limited to *part* of the mid-West.

general presumption were that nearly all mergers, as well as involving the large, but more diffused and harder to quantify detriment of making the structure of markets less competitive, also actively achieved performance benefits. That there has been such a presumption is clear, for example, from the President's February speech[1]:—'In general, mergers are desirable if they lead to better management or genuine economies of scale without eliminating workable competition. In my view, more often than not in Britain mergers will fulfil this condition.' My argument has been that the general evidence, as well as the more specific results to be found in recent reports of the Commission, does not support such a presumption. Indeed, the Board itself has quietly retreated. It now claims only that 'as was expected, the majority of mergers appear to be neutral from the point of view of the public interest' (*Mergers*, para. 88). This shift in view is illustrated dramatically in the statement made by the President in introducing *Mergers*. Although the President claimed that the recent merger movement 'had been on balance beneficial', he went on to take some of the credit for 'taking the fever out of the merger movement'. The reasons he gave for thinking that we might now somehow be getting too much of a good thing do not diminish the inconsistency, since they seem to apply equally well to the mergers which have already taken place.[2]

Thus it seems to me that the time has now come to bring the procedure more into line with the evidence, and with the view of it apparently now taken by the Board. That requires that where the potential structural detriment from a merger is greatest it should need to be offset by the greatest performance improvements. Thus the benefits alleged to flow from the majority of mergers involving *large* companies should be examined more thoroughly by an economically sophisticated body, with more expert staff, asking quantitative questions, all in a framework where much more visible weight is given to the long-run and irreversible potential detriments which are liable to flow from a weakening, under the impact of privately

---

[1] See *Mergers*, p. 58.

[2] 'First, large scale mergers can have social consequences which are a matter of public concern. Secondly, greater absolute size is by no means a guarantee of greater efficiency. Thirdly, we need to keep a proper size-distribution of firms in the economy; in particular, we do not want to see efficient medium-sized companies continuously swallowed up in a fever of take-over activity. Fourthly there are certain obvious limitations on the judgment of the market in the case of contested take-over bids.' (*Board of Trade Journal*, 6 August, 1969, p. 346.)

controlled monoliths, of that 'competitive environment' which the President wishes to maintain.

One way would be to combine my suggestions for changing the question in all merger cases (see p. 129 above) and my suggestion for issuing guidelines even within the present framework (see p. 129 above) with a shift in the onus of proof in the mergers involving the biggest companies. Thus where a company already large enough to be in the top 100 companies, say (which currently implies that its capital employed is around £50m.), proposes to undertake a qualifying merger (or where a merger would take smaller companies into this size class) the procedure should require the companies to convince the Commission that there would be net potential benefit—and not, as now, that the Commission was able to convince itself that there was non-negative potential benefit. For the very biggest companies, say the top twenty-five, with capital employed of about £200m. or more, the evidence suggests that economies of scale must already be fully within their reach. Here there is a case for saying that further growth by vertical or horizontal merger should be assumed to be always against the public interest, and there should be a complete prohibition—with perhaps an appeal on the grounds that really spectacular net benefit could be established. However, to avoid having two standards in one Act, and to avoid the discontinuity in treatment that would be involved for a company moving from rank 26 to rank 25, roughly this result could be achieved without introducing an explicitly *per se* prohibition by an Act worded somewhat as follows:—

'The Board may refer any qualifying merger to the Commission to decide whether it would be in the public interest. (The size of assets qualification might perhaps be set a little higher than at present. The monopoly test should remain.) The Board may instruct the Commission in any particular class of cases that the onus of proof should be on the companies; and may further indicate that in a particular class of cases the onus would not be discharged unless "substantial" net benefit to the public were demonstrated.' The Board would then be empowered to issue guidelines, from time to time, for the classes of merger which would be treated in these special ways. Thus they might be of the form: 'In general' the Board would refer to the Commission *all* cases where a merger involves companies already in 'roughly' the top hundred companies ranked by capital employed (or an actual amount of capital could be specified; or sales could be used instead), or where a merger would take a company into this class; further, the Board would specify that the onus of proof would be shifted to the companies in these cases. Further, the Board would 'in general' specify that 'substantial' benefit should be shown for mergers involving 'roughly' the top twenty-five.[1] In due course these guidelines on the size of the acquiring company could be modified by guidelines on market shares, so that large companies in an unusually competitive environment would not be automatically referred, while smaller companies with tight market control would be. The sizes, and the definitions of market shares, could then themselves be altered with the passage of time.

With such a structure all qualifying mergers involving the top hundred companies would nearly automatically go to the Commission for an answer[2]; and the Board would then have more time to devote to the mergers involving companies not quite so large; in deciding whether *prima facie* they should be referred the Board would then in future (because now for all referred mergers the question would be whether they were positively in the public interest) give much more weight to the presence of potential benefits and less to the apparent absence of detriments. The fact that the Board's investigation in these cases would inevitably be more superficial than the Commission's would be an acceptable price to pay to avoid overloading the Commission; and a 'wrong' answer on these smaller mergers costs the public interest less.

Note that these changes would not mean that the top twenty-five, or the top hundred had to stagnate. They could still grow, as they do

---

[1] Because the size of the *acquiring* company is not relevant in the present Act, there is no up-to-date official guide to the number of mergers in each of my proposed size divisions. Statistics are given showing the breakdown of acquisitions by size class—but the size structure of acquirers is not now given. The last official information seems to be that given in *Economic Trends*, No. 114, April 1963, in 'Acquisitions and amalgamations of quoted companies 1954–61':—'The very large companies—those with assets of £25m. or more numbering [in 1960] 98 out of a total of about 2,600 quoted companies—accounted for about half of all acquisition expenditure . . .'. These very large companies acquired 167 quoted companies (at an average cost of £3½m.) and 208 unquoted (at an average cost of £1m.). Thus the top hundred companies then were making qualifying acquisitions at a rate of less than thirty a year. The pace has quickened since, but the administrative task of designing a structure which would enable the Commission to investigate *all* such mergers is not manifestly impossible.

[2] This retention of a performance test in the new framework would still leave the U.K. with a less stringent system than the U.S. already has now.

now, by expanding their sales in rivalry with other companies, and without reducing the number of sellers in the market.

Note also that the policy suggestions for changing the question, for publishing guidelines for the cases to be referred, and for shifting the onus, are separable from one another. My view is that the time is ripe to make all of them: but each of them individually would be an improvement. For instance, a decision to introduce a guideline that mergers by the top hundred would always be referred to the Commission within the present Act would, even by itself, have a desirable effect.

Conclusion

To conclude, there is no doubt that U.K. industry needs to continue to change; and no doubt that in many cases that change should include an increase in scale—of companies by merger, as well as of plants with or without merger. But the evidence is that we have now reached, if not already passed, the point where concern for the preservation of the structural conditions for effective rivalry should make us take the risk of insisting on a much closer examination of future mergers contemplated by those companies which are already large and dominant in their industries. I would hope that such a changed policy on mergers would not prevent there being more frequent references of existing monopolies, designed to allow the Commission to check how far the bright hopes promised for giants, new and old, have in fact been realised. These seem to me to be two policy shifts which are required if the management of this aspect of economic policy is to be nearer the ideal.

8

Cost-Benefit Analysis

Prof. Alan Williams*

Public bodies are frequently being exhorted to emulate the efficient practices of private enterprise and cut out waste, prune down the bloated army of faceless tea-swilling civil servants, and replace them with people who are imbued with a more ruthless attitude to cost-reducing innovation, bred by prolonged exposure to the rigours of the market place and the consequent need to make profits in order to survive. It is true that not all observers of the current scene are of this view, indeed, one popular weekly recently expressed the very opposite sentiment, to wit:

'It would be difficult to argue—though some industrialists would try—that this country is dynamically managed in industry but in-efficiently administered by government. Our civil service is the envy, our board-rooms the scorn, of Europe or North America.' (*New Statesman*, 8th July, 1969).

I do not propose to enter this particular arena, if for no better reason than that any third party joining the fray is likely to be severely gored by both protagonists. I propose instead to play the role of the man in the ivory tower pontificating upon the fallibility of those on the one side who fall too easily into the mistaken belief that government is like business, when it isn't; and of those, on the other side, who believe that government is not like business, when it is.

My basic theme is that there are indeed useful techniques which government can learn from private industry, especially in the field of investment appraisal, just as there is much that business can learn from government (though this will not be my concern here). But even if every governmental agency were a paragon of 'best practice' in this sense, there would still be important considerations which would need to be brought into the analysis for governmental pur-poses but which the private sector can afford to ignore. On occasion

* Professor in the Department of Economics, University of York.

these additional considerations will lead to outcomes which appear incomprehensible, or even plain wrong, if judged by narrow private sector criteria. My objective in this paper is to explain why this may be so, in order that discussion of these controversial matters may proceed on a somewhat higher plane than indicated in my deliberately provocative opening remarks.

My chief concern will be with investment appraisal rather than with other aspects of efficiency, although much of what I have to say would apply to appraising the efficiency of current operations too. I limit myself to investment problems because they are more spectacular, and hence provide a better vehicle for conveying the message I want to get across. It is also in the field of capital formation that the quantitative role of the public sector (including nationalised industries) is most noticeable (the public sector is responsible for roughly half of all gross fixed capital formation in the economy). The essence of all investment appraisal is to determine what the overall situation of the investor would be with and without the investment in question, and with and without any feasible alternative investments which are competitive or complementary to it. It is an area of enquiry which is easy to describe in these general terms, more difficult to formulate in detail, and much more difficult to give specific quantitative content to; yet specific quantitative content it has to have if it is to impose a rigorous discipline on woolly thinking, and that is my understanding of what a 'scientific' approach to a problem means.

Efficient Private-Sector Investment Appraisal

The method of investment appraisal currently being promulgated as 'best practice' in the private sector is the 'discounted cash flow' (DCF) technique. It involves three basic elements:

(1) Estimating a revenue stream;

(2) Estimating an expenditure stream;

(3) Applying a discounting procedure to render (1) and (2) commensurable.

Then if the discounted 'present value' of the revenue stream is greater than that of the expenditure stream, the investment is worth doing, i.e. will yield a net profit.

I will describe each element at greater length in turn in order to bring out the essential characteristics of each.

In estimating the revenue stream the two features which are stressed are:

(a) that only actual cash receipts into the firm are to be counted; and

(b) that they are to be accurately placed in time at the date on which they will occur.

The stress on actual cash receipts is based on the notion that building up a long and impressive list of 'accounts due' from customers is not going to help the shareholders much, whereas an inflow of hard cash is, so it is no good counting success (as a salesman might) by the volume of orders taken, or even the volume of goods invoiced out; the acid test is 'when will the cash roll in?' Up until then the firm is simply providing trade credit which helps to finance other people's businesses, and these 'loans' are usually interest-free into the bargain! The stress on accurately dating the expected time of receipt will be of obvious significance in this respect, since the later in time any particular receipt occurs, the greater the 'interest-free loan' implied.

On the expenditure side similar considerations apply: items are charged when they have to be paid for, not when the goods are ordered, or delivered, or even (necessarily) when the account nominally falls due. Analogously, taxation enters when the actual tax payments are due, not when the liability to tax arises. But insistence on recording cash outlays as and when they take place does not always mean that they occur *later* than in more conventional accounting practice. For instance, if a piece of machinery is purchased for cash in a lump sum, the whole cash payment goes in at the point of time it is made. . . it is not 'spread' over the expected life of the asset as with conventional depreciation allowances, because these latter are simply a device for apportioning capital costs period by period for purposes of striking annual balance sheets and profit and loss statements, and have no relevance to the problem of determining the profitability over its whole lifetime of a particular investment. Thus although the 'cash flow' approach seems very simple and straightforward at first sight, it does mark a significant departure from the notions of profit and loss upon which much accounting practice is based, and can therefore lead to results which puzzle those whose thinking has been conditioned in this way.

The discounting procedure is the element which, in my experience, people have the greatest difficulty in comprehending. At a merely arithmetical level, its meaning could be explained in the following roundabout way: If the rate of interest is 10%, then by the familiar mysteries of compound interest we can all (though perhaps with some difficulty) calculate that £100 this year will be worth £110 next year, £121 the following year, and after that (if you are getting a bit slow like me) it is necessary to consult more agile minds (like any sixth formers we may have in the household) in order to work out whether the next figure in the series is 132·1 or 131·2 or 133·1 or whatever. Discounting is the opposite of compounding, for it tells you what £100 due at some specified time would be worth to you at some *earlier* date. Thus £100 due next year is worth £90·9 this year if the interest rate is 10%, because if you had £90·9 now and invested it at 10% you could turn it into £100 next year. By the same token, £100 due in two years' time would be worth only £82·6 now, because by compounding £82·6 at 10% for two years it would amount to £100. For those who prefer formulae to arithmetic, the present value (V) of a sum (S) due in n years' time is given by the expression:

$$V = \frac{S}{(1+r)^n}$$

where r is the rate of interest expressed as a fraction (i.e. 10% = 0·1).

The arithmetic of discounting is not the key issue, however, for it does not *justify* the process or *explain* what is at stake, but merely how you do it. The justification for discounting is that cash invested in any project could be used in other ways (e.g. placed in the bank to earn interest or invested in other projects, or used to buy shares in other companies, or distributed to shareholders), and that the most valuable alternative use should be taken as establishing the minimum acceptable rate-of-return on the project in question. This minimum rate of return is the rate of interest (r) that must go into discounting process. If the firm places a low value on the alternative uses of funds, then the rate will be low, and more projects will prove acceptable to it than would be accepted by a firm using a high discount rate. The method of calculating the appropriate discount rate is therefore of considerable significance.

The general view is that it should represent the rate of return that shareholders can expect to get if the proceeds are distributed to them and if they then invest in a representative portfolio selection on the

Stock Exchange. This figure is more difficult to compute than it seems, partly because of taxation complications, partly because current stock exchange valuations and yields do not perfectly reflect the earning capacity of different assets because of differences in riskiness, varying assessments of prospects, etc. But at bottom it is nevertheless the earning prospects of a firm's shareholders if the cash were distributed to them which sets the floor to the prospective rate-of-return acceptable on projects within the firm, on the grounds that the firm has no right to use shareholders' resources in ways inferior to those which the shareholders can organise directly for themselves.

What the discounting process then does is to reduce to a single capital sum each of the two cash flows (revenue and expenditure). These two 'Present Values' are then compared, and if the Present Value of the Revenues exceeds the Present Value of the Expenditures, the *Net Present Value* (the difference between them) is positive, and the investment is worth undertaking, because the rate of return is greater than the minimum required. If the two Present Values are equal, Net Present Value is zero, and the investment yields exactly the minimum required rate but no more. Clearly, if the Net Present Value is negative, the project does not meet the test, and will be rejected. This, in the barest outline, and stripped of many important complications, is what efficient investment appraisal in the private sector is all about. (Those seeking a fuller description are recommended to read the second edition of the NEDC booklet *Investment Appraisal* (HMSO, 1967), and the further references given therein.)

What relevance has this for the Public Sector?

There are plenty of public sector activities to which this technique of *financial* appraisal would be relevant and useful, notably in the fields covered by the nationalised industries. Indeed it is official policy to encourage the use of these techniques there (as witness the White Paper, *Nationalised Industries: A Review of Economic and Financial Objectives*, Cmnd 3437, November 1967). One major complication, however, is that a nationalised industry is much more constrained in its price-fixing behaviour than is a private firm, and may also be expected (in the public interest) to refrain from using its market power to maximise profits. Thus the actual profitability of nationalised industries is not a reliable indicator of the efficiency of their investment appraisal, for such efficiency may, quite deliberately, be reflected in lower prices and hence lower revenues instead. This does not render the D.C.F. technique inappropriate, however, for it will still be necessary for the industry to minimise its costs, even though its prices and revenues may be closely regulated for other reasons, and to do this it will need to have efficient means for appraising the impact on the finances of the organisation of alternative means of producing the required output.

But, as the White Paper recognises, it is not necessarily enough to ensure that nationalised industries' rate-of-return on investment projects is at least equal to 'the average rate of return in real terms looked for on low-risk projects in the private sector in recent years'. This minimum rate of return, known as the 'test discount rate', was originally set at 8%, and increased to 10% in August 1969, and is the rate now used by all nationalised industries in the discounting procedure described above. It is designed to ensure that the public sector does not use capital resources which could be more profitably used in the private sector. The relationships between the test rate of discount, the pricing policy of nationalised industries, and the setting of financial targets for those industries are explored further in Michael Posner's paper in this volume.

The admitted inadequacy of this minimum financial rate of return as a cut-off rate for investment appraisal in the public sector becomes evident when considerations other than commercial viability enter the picture in a significant way. As the White Paper puts it:

'The economic value of investments cannot always be measured by reference to the financial return to the industry concerned. Many investments also produce social costs and benefits which can in principle be valued in financial terms and which, when taken into account, will provide a good economic justification for them.' (para 14). It is at this point that financial appraisal gives way to economic appraisal, and discounted-cash-flow needs to be transformed into cost-benefit analysis.

The essence of this transformation is easy enough to state in general terns, by going back to the three basic elements of the D.C.F. technique and identifying their analogues in cost-benefit analysis:

Financial Appraisal by DCF technique	Economic Appraisal by Cost-Benefit Analysis
Estimate a revenue stream Estimate an expenditure stream Apply a discounting procedure	Estimate a benefit stream Estimate a cost stream Apply a discounting procedure

This apparently slight change in terminology belies the radical nature of the conceptual change that has been wrought. Substituting benefits for revenues implies a much wider scope for analysis than mere cash flows, as we shall see. Likewise, the substitution of 'costs' for 'expenditures' is more than a semantic point, for the economists' notion of 'costs' and the accountants' notion of 'expenditures' can be poles apart, again as we shall see. Finally, the discounting procedure, though arithmetically the same, has a very different conceptual basis, simply because the 'shareholders' in governmental enterprises constitute the community at large, and it is not self-evident what rate of discount represents the minimum rate of return they would be prepared to accept, nor how it should be calculated. This is a highly controversial area of current dispute between professional economists, and since the issues at stake are rather complicated I propose to leave it on one side today. Those who are gluttons for punishment, and would like to catch the flavour of that dispute, may care to look at the recent C.A.S. Occasional Paper No. 11, which I wrote jointly with H. G. Walsh, called *Current Issues in Cost-Benefit Analysis* (H.M.S.O., 1969).

In order to bring out as sharply as possible the differences between financial appraisal of a D.C.F. type and economic appraisal by cost-benefit analysis, I propose to present, for your examination and comment, three 'exhibits', each of which has been cunningly selected to illustrate an important point.

I must stress that although the factual under-pinning of each of my three illustrative 'exhibits' has been distorted in order to heighten the dramatic effect, the issue which I thereby highlight in each case is a real and significant one, and I would be sorry if anyone were to be misled by this particular mode of exposition into thinking that the problems I pose arise only because I have presented them in such a simplified set of circumstances. Just as the natural sciences proceed by abstraction and simplification, so does economics!

Exhibit 1

The London Underground Network

Suppose that it is proposed to add a new link to the London Underground Network, and that it is decided in advance that the fares on this new section will be at the same rate per mile as on existing lines. On this basis estimates are made of the numbers of travellers who will switch to the new link, distinguishing those who would otherwise have travelled by other bits of the network, by bus, by car, or not at all. Suppose further that on this basis the present value of the estimated fare revenues from users of the new link is less than the present value of the costs of the new link, should the link be provided or not? On a strictly financial appraisal, the answer would be 'no', especially since some of the revenue 'gained' by the new link would simply represent revenue 'lost' to other parts of the transport undertaking (i.e. bus routes and other tube lines).

But now consider the problem in a slightly wider context. The new link provides benefits for people other than those who use it. It cuts journey times for surface transport users at peak hours by relieving road congestion, and these time savings are worth money, as are the reductions in vehicle operating costs. These benefits are real benefits to the community, even though they will not be reflected in fare revenue to the transport undertaking. When added to the other 'returns' from the investment they may be large enough to make a *financially unprofitable* investment into an *economically beneficial* one.

The case may be pushed a stage further, for it could be argued that attempts to make such an investment financially profitable may make it economically *un*beneficial! This could happen if, as a result of the 'losses' that were being made on the line, it were decided to raise fares, hence reducing the extent to which people diverted to the new link from surface transport. The additional costs of congestion on the surface might then outweigh the cost savings on the link itself, and far from improving the situation might engender the paradoxical result that the overall costs to the community now outweighed the overall benefits.

Thus from my first exhibit I conclude that there are instances where the benefits accruing to people who do not contribute directly to the revenues of the investing organisation may be sufficient to outweigh the apparent excess of costs over benefits as measured by that body's expenditures and revenues respectively.

Exhibit 2

Nuclear versus Coal-fired Power Stations

There seems little doubt that nuclear power is the fuel of the future, but is it the right fuel source for Britain to be investing in *now*? Suppose that the CEGB. requires some additional capacity, and it can either be provided by installing a coal-fired generator or by a nuclear-powered one. Let us further suppose that despite its high initial capital costs, the nuclear-powered station turns out to be cheaper in the long run (i.e. the present value of its cost stream when discounted at the appropriate interest rate is lower than that of the coal-fired station) because of its very low running costs. (Since both power stations generate the same amount of electricity, sold at the same price, we can ignore the revenue side in this comparison.) On a strictly financial appraisal, the answer would be 'go nuclear!' but (as you will doubtless already have guessed) I am going to twist the situation round so that the correct answer will be 'stick with coal!'

The feature of the situation which could enable me to do this (if the facts were as I am going to suppose them to be) is that the coal industry is a declining industry, in which many former miners are becoming redundant with little prospect of re-employment. In order to simplify my argument, I am going to distort the picture here by assuming that none of them get re-employed, which, happily, is not the case.

A basic principle in economics is that the true cost of using any resource is the most valuable alternative use to which it could be put, because that is what is being forgone, that is the 'sacrifice' which is being made, and that is what a 'cost' ultimately is. This principle was used earlier in arguing that the true cost of using capital in a firm is the return which shareholders can get on that capital themselves. This notion is known generally in economics as 'opportunity cost', i.e. the cost in terms of alternative opportunities forgone.

If we apply this concept of 'opportunity cost' to coal miners, we can say that since they will (by hypothesis) be unemployed if not hewing coal, then no alternative use of the labour is in fact being forgone, and the true cost of their labour to the community is zero. (As an aside, it may be added that if being unemployed is considered a bad thing *per se*, and not just a waste of resources, then we could go further and say that having them hew coal would be regarded as a *negative* cost, i.e. as a positive benefit, quite apart from the value of the coal.) In this view of the situation, any wage payments made to them are merely 'transfer payments' (like social security benefits), and although they represent cash outflows in any D.C.F. calculations made by the NCB., they are not true costs to the community as defined above in accordance with one of the fundamental principles of economics.

Returning to the power station problem, a cost-benefit analyst, looking at the facts as assumed for purposes of this argument, would say that the cost of coal has to be reduced by disregarding the component representing expenditure on miners' labour, and it would be this lower, notional, coal price which should be used in the calculations comparing nuclear and coal-fired power stations. It could be that it would swing the answer the opposite way to what the financial appraisal indicated, and the conclusion of the economic appraisal would then be to stick with coal because of the consequent unemployment of miners if the nuclear powered station were selected.

Let me hasten to add that this does not imply that cost-benefit analysis is the enemy of technical progress, or that it can be used to prop up any declining industry indefinitely, or that the CEGB and the NCB should become out-stations of the Department of Health and Social Security. All that I am saying is that in economic terms it may be advantageous for the community as a whole to disregard the effects of a particular investment upon the finances of one agency (in this case the CEGB), and to require it *not* to do something which, within its own notions of commercial viability, it would regard as the profitable thing for it to do, and to substitute in its place something which it would regard as 'unprofitable'.

Exhibit 3

Trunk Road Improvements

My third exhibit is of rather a different kind, being concerned with projects which do not yield revenues (in the conventional sense) at all. I refer to major improvements in the inter-urban trunk road system, like road widening schemes, bypasses, new alignments, etc., but not totally new elements like motorways. The problem here is to devise a means of 'simulating' a rate of return, so that conventional techniques of investment appraisal can be applied to determine which projects should be done and which rejected. The *costs* of such road improvements will not be examined further here, but will be taken (for the sake of argument) as properly represented by the actual cash outlays entailed.

The potential *benefits* from a road improvement are:

(a) Reduction in vehicle operating costs.

(b) Time savings;

(c) Reduced accident rates;

The first item needs no further elaboration, and most people will concede in principle that the second item (time saving) is worth money, though there is plenty of room for dispute about how one should set about valuing it and what its actual 'price' should be. These little difficulties I brush aside simply because I am anxious to get to grips with bigger ones. In my view the biggest difficulties lie in the evaluation of reduced accident rates, and it is upon this element in the calculation that I propose to concentrate.

The benefits flowing from reduced accident rates can be split into the following components:

(i) reduced damage to vehicles;

(ii) reduced damage to people;

(iii) reduced disruption, congestion, etc., due to accidents but suffered by non-participants.

Item (iii) resolves once more into time savings, vehicle operating costs, etc., and item (i) is also fairly straightforward in its economic implications. It is item (ii), concerning 'damage to people', that is the tricky item to deal with. It has some economic and some non-economic attributes. The economic attributes consist of the costs of providing medical services, ambulance services, etc., for survivors, and the costs of providing the conventional apparatus for the disposal of the bodies of those who do not survive, and the costs, in terms of real resources, of community provision for dependents (such as orphanages). But the community also loses their productive effort, which may (in the case of a member of the working population) be reflected in the GNP statistics, or which may not be so counted conventionally (e.g. housewives' services) yet be of considerable economic value to the community (as we discover when we need to find a substitute for them!) There is therefore an item for 'output forgone' to be included in the cost of road accidents when death or disablement (albeit temporary) of people who would otherwise have been providing economically valuable services is involved. This element in the computation will indicate that it 'costs' the community relatively more if an 17-year-old male motor-cyclist gets killed than if an elderly pedestrian is killed. This inference is not one to be shirked or brushed under the carpet as distasteful to humane people, for it simply states a fact, in the same sense that it is a fact (however distasteful) that x thousand people are killed on the roads each year, of whom $y\%$ could have been saved if we (or they) had done z (or not done z).

But all the items mentioned so far are what might be called 'cold-blooded' costs. They do not include pain, grief, or suffering, either by the casualties themselves or by their nearest and dearest. Let us now turn to these 'non-economic attributes' and see how they might be brought into the picture in a quantitative way, for, it is important to try to do this if we are to avoid the risk that they will either be ignored or treated in a capricious and haphazard way. One possible way to get a money value placed on these 'warm-blooded' costs is to look at court awards for damages, because the courts are asked to assess, on behalf of the community at large, the money value to be placed on 'loss of marital happiness', the mental anguish of parents of deformed babies, and similar intangible kinds of suffering, which come very close to what we are after. It could therefore be argued that it would be inconsistent to approve of one system of awards in one sphere and deny their relevance to corresponding circumstances elsewhere, where the only difference might be that in the one case there are legal grounds for a civil action but in the other case there are not.

It may be argued, however, that the courts are really very ill-equipped to carry out this function, and that their admitted inadequacy is tolerable only because the relatively few cases they have to deal with do not warrant the major upheaval that would be necessary to place them in a position to do better. But if some sum of money is going to be used in all investment calculations involving these phenomena, it would be better to go back to fundamentals and get a direct social valuation for this specific purpose. I have some sympathy with this view, but I can see no other way of getting such a valuation except by an explicit statement of policy by the government. To this end I would welcome an informed public debate on this issue, so that policy makers had some idea of how people felt about it, and whether we are devoting too much or too little of our resources to this end (i.e. whether the 'price' implicit inadvertently in current decisions is too high or too low). Indeed, I would welcome discussion of this same problem in the much more general context of our policy on resource allocation in all the fields in which the avoidance of death and injury and illness is involved, for instance with respect to the National Health Service, industrial safety, air pollution, etc.

There are doubtless some amongst you who are thinking, if not muttering out loud, that the ultimate horror envisaged by science fiction writers is already upon us, in the shape of the cold, calculating, heartless, sub-human computer (in the guise of the economist) placing a money value on human suffering, and indeed on life itself. Such an emotional reaction, though understandable, is neither helpful nor tenable, because whether we like it or not, there is a limit to how much of our resources we are willing to devote to prolonging life or reducing suffering. If there were not such a limit, our entire GNP would be devoted to keeping alive the starving and the sick, and all the many other expenditures which raise the quality of life for the healthy would have to be sacrificed. Since such decisions have to be made, it is better that they be made rationally, by which I mean calmly and in full knowledge of the consequences, for we shall then, as a community, be better able to achieve our general, social objectives. For instance, if one of our objectives is to prolong life, then if we place an explicit value on the postponement of death for anybody by one year, and use it consistently for all activities promoting that objective, we shall prolong life more than if we devote thousands of pounds to saving one life per year on the railways, while refusing to spend a few hundred pounds to save a similar life on the roads. Unless we come out in the open and specify what sum we are willing to devote to this purpose, we must expect haphazard and inefficient investment decisions to be made in this respect.

Conclusions

Let me now draw the threads together. My three exhibits were presented in order to demonstrate situations (1) where cost-benefit analysis would tell you to do something which private sector financial appraisal would tell you you *ought not* to do, (2) where cost-benefit analysis would tell you *not* to do something which private sector financial appraisal would tell you you *ought* to do, and (3) where cost-benefit analysis takes on board such a wide range of considerations that we are led to confront questions of valuation which, in their private capacities, people do not need to confront, and in some cases would prefer to ignore. For all of these reasons I would not expect cost-benefit analysis to be a particularly popular technique, for it disturbs pre-conceived notions of what is meant by 'efficiency', and it forces us to be explicit and precise where we are frequently vague and woolly. But whether it proves 'popular' in this sense or not, I believe it to be both necessary and useful in improving the quality of investment decisions in the public sector.

The Role of Local Authorities in the Growth of Public Expenditure in the United Kingdom

Dr. A. E. Holmans*

Introduction

In an earlier paper[1] it was shown that civil public expenditure in the United Kingdom has been rising substantially faster than GNP, both in money and real terms, since the mid-1950s. For a time the rise in civil expenditure was offset by a decline in defence expenditure; but when in the early 1960s the fall in defence expenditure came to a halt, the growth of civil expenditure did not slacken; on the contrary it appears to have accelerated. The continued growth of civil expenditure, in relation to GNP, in the 1960s was accompanied by an increase in the weight of taxation, and so was at variance with the trends discerned by Professors Peacock and Wiseman in their analysis of trends in public expenditure in the United Kingdom up to 1950.[2]

The purpose of this paper is to examine the role of local authorities in the rapid growth of civil public expenditure since the mid-1950s. The rise in local authorities' expenditure, and its corollary, a rapid rise in rates, have been widely commented on. Ratepayers' discontent, aggravated by the impact of the 1963 revaluation, led to a thorough investigation of the incidence of domestic rates[3]; and in

* Senior Economic Adviser, Ministry of Housing and Local Government. The views expressed are those of the author, and must not be taken to represent the views of his Department.

[1] A. E. Holmans, 'The growth of public expenditure in the United Kingdom since 1950', *Manchester School*, Vol. XXXVI (1968), pp. 313–27.

[2] A. T. Peacock and J. Wiseman, *The Growth of Public Expenditure in the United Kingdom*, Princeton University Press, Publication, 1961.

[3] *Report of Committee of Inquiry into the Impact of Rates on Housholds*, 1965 (Cmnd 2582).

the White Paper on local government finance in 1966[1] the rapid rise in expenditure and rates since the mid-1950s was remarked on. Among the sharpest criticisms was that by Professor Sir John Hicks. In his analysis of the causes of the economic difficulties that preceded the deflationary measures of July 1966 he concluded that an unduly rapid rise in public expenditure was the principal cause of the excess demand that led to the crisis; and that within the growth of public expenditure 'the immediate problem is very largely one of local expenditure'.[2] Professor Hicks noted that a considerable part of the increase was accounted for by education, where national policies limit the area of local authorities' discretion; but of the rest of the growth of local expenditure, he wrote, 'It is dreadful to think how much of our national deficit is ultimately traceable to local expenditure on civic amenities'.[3]

This paper seeks to identify the factors that account for the changing balance between Central and local government expenditure, and the changes in the total and composition of local authorities' expenditure. The effect of the growth of local authorities' expenditure on the economy, the subject of primary interest to Professor Hicks in his pamphlet cited above, is not considered here. But brief reference is made to the implications of the growth of local authority expenditure for the use of variations in public expenditure as a means of managing the economy.

The scale of local authorities' expenditure in relation to expenditure by the Central government by itself signifies very little about the division of power and responsibilities. A faster rise in local authorities' expenditure than in Central government expenditure is not proof of an increase in local authorities' exercise of autonomous responsibility. The relationship between Central and local government in determining policy which is carried into effect through local authority expenditure (in part financed from Exchequer grants) is not examined here; no inferences are drawn about to what extent, if at all, the faster growth of local authorities' expenditure means that they have gained in power relative to the Central government.

The first part of the paper relates the post-1950 developments in very summary terms to previous trends. In the next part, develop-

---

[1] *Local Government Finance in England and Wales* (Cmnd 2923).

[2] Sir John Hicks, *After the Boom,* Institute of Economic Affairs, London, 1966, p. 15.

[3] Hicks, *op cit.,* p. 16.

ments between 1950 and 1967 are analysed in more detail, to pick out the elements that made up the total change in local government expenditure in absolute terms, in relation to total public expenditure, and in relation to GNP. The third part deals with the composition of the growth of expenditure, and the final sections comment on the role of local authorities' expenditure in the management of the economy, and on future prospects.

The Growth of Local Expenditure: the Long Term Perspective

In their analysis of trends in public expenditure in the United Kingdom, Peacock and Wiseman discerned a 'concentration process' whereby the Central government's share of total expenditure, excluding defence, interest on war debts, and other war-related expenditure increased.[1] This concentration process, like the 'displacement effect'[2] was found to be associated with the two World Wars. One point to be commented on accordingly is whether the war-time 'concentration process' has been reversed to any extent.

It is necessary to make a brief reference to problems of definition and coverage. For years before 1950, the expenditure estimates used are taken directly from Peacock and Wiseman without any adjustment. The definitions they used[3] are very similar to those used by the Central Statistical Office in the annual issues of *National Income and Expenditure*[4] which are the source of the estimates for the period since 1950. Such differences as do exist are not sufficient to impair materially the comparability between the aggregates shown in Table 5 below.

For the period after 1950, the definitions and coverage for total public expenditure are as in the earlier article[5], with two additional adjustments. In 1966 and 1967 Selective Employment Tax paid in respect of Central and local government employees, and in 1967 investment grants, are included in public expenditure. Investment grants replaced investment allowances. The latter, being tax reliefs,

---

[1] Peacock and Wiseman, *op. cit.,* pp. 29–30 and Ch. 6. This reference, and all others, are to the 2nd edition (Allen and Unwin, 1967).

[2] The sharp jumps in the level of civil expenditure relative to GNP. See Holmans, *op. cit.,* pp. 313–15, for discussion.

[3] Peacock and Wiseman, *op. cit.,* pp. 158–61.

[4] Central Statistical Office, *National Accounts Statistics: Sources and Methods,* HMSO (1968), Chapters IX, X, and XI.

[5] Holmans, *op. cit.,* p. 317.

were not included in totals of expenditure; and to maintain comparability investment grants are excluded also. As part of the machinery for collecting SET, Central government and local authorities pay SET along with employers' National Insurance contributions, but their SET payments are subsequently refunded, except in respect of employees employed on new construction work. Public authorities' expenditure is shown gross of SET in the national income accounts, with a corresponding entry for refunds on the revenue side. This has the effect of inflating expenditure at current prices in comparison with previous years, and SET payments that are subsequently refunded are excluded.

'Local authorities' as defined in the National Income accounts is a term with very wide coverage. It includes not only territorial authorities ranging from counties and county boroughs to parishes, but also special-purpose bodies like river authorities, water boards (ranging in size from the Metropolitan Water Board downwards), and certain public trading bodies like the Port of London Authority and the Mersey Docks and Harbour Board. The distinction between such bodies and public corporations is a fine one; and there seems no incongruity about including with local authorities the new town Development Corporations, the New Towns Commission, and the Scottish Special Housing Association. The reasons for including these public corporations with Central and local government were outlined in the earlier article.[1]

The growth of local authorities' expenditure, compared with Central government expenditure and GNP, all in terms of current prices, over the sixty years prior to 1950, is shown in Table 5. The comparison is made both in terms of total public expenditure and of total expenditure other than 'war-related' expenditure (i.e. defence, interest on the National Debt, and war pensions).

Even before World War I, local authorities' expenditure was rising considerably faster than GNP. After World War I local authorities acquired new powers and duties, notably in the fields of education and housing, with the result that their expenditure in the early 1920s was considerably higher, in relation to GNP, than before the War. The reduction in the local authorities' share of total public expenditure was nearly all due to higher expenditure by the Central government on defence and debt interest. There was little of Peacock and

[1] Holmans, *op. cit.*, p. 317.

Table 5: *Central and Local Government Expenditure in Relation to GNP, 1890–1950*

	1890	1913	1924	1937	1950
Total Expenditure	(% *of GNP*)				
Central Government	5·5	6·8	15·9	15·9	29·9
Local Authorities	3·4	5·5	7·8	9·8	9·1
Total Expenditure other than War Related					
Central Government	1·5	2·4	4·2	5·3	16·7
Local Authorities	3·4	5·5	7·8	9·8	6·1
Expenditure by Local Authorities	(% *of Total Public Expenditure*)				
All Expenditure	38	45	33	38	23
All Expenditure other than War-Related	70	70	65	62	35

Source: Calculated from data in Peacock and Wiseman. *The Growth of Public Expenditure in the United Kingdom*, Tables A–2, A–5, A–7, and A–20.

Wiseman's 'concentration process' in civil expenditure, for the principal expansions of public services following World War I were in the local authority field.

After World War II events took a different course. The setting up of the National Health Service and the expansion of National Insurance substantially increased civil expenditure by the Central government, and at the same time important functions previously undertaken by local authorities were transferred elsewhere. Public assistance, a local authority function since Elizabeth I's reign, was transferred to the National Assistance Board; local authorities' mental and general hospitals were transferred to the National Health Service; and local authorities' gas and electricity undertakings were nationalised along with the rest of the industries. The transfer of these services had a substantial impact; in 1937 total expenditure on hospitals and asylums, poor relief, and capital expenditure by local authority gas and electricity undertakings totalled about £113m.[1], equal to 22% of total expenditure by local authorities and 2·2% of GNP. The 'concentration process' worked powerfully, both through

[1] Expenditure figures taken from B. R. Mitchell and Phyllis Deane, *Abstract of British Historical Statistics*, Cambridge University Press, 1962. Tables Public Finance 10, 11, 12 and 13.

an expansion of Central government activity, and a diminution of
the activities of local authorities.

In the inter-war years such growth as took place in the local
authorities' share of total expenditure was due to a fall in interest on
the National Debt; the Central government's share of ordinary civil
expenditure increased slightly. But after 1950, events took a different
course; as is shown in Table 6, the local authority share of civil
expenditure increased considerably. There were fluctuations, and
given the extent to which these were due to changes in housing
policy (discussed in more detail below) it is useful to show the comparison also in terms of civil domestic expenditure excluding housing.
Domestic civil expenditure is defined to exclude debt interest; this is
clearly proper for interest on the National Debt, for when the
Central government's receipts of interest on loans to public corporations and local authorities (for whom it acts as a financial inter-
mediary) are netted off, all that remains is interest on war debts.
For local authorities, the position is more difficult; their debts were
incurred to finance the acquisition of real assets, and for that reason
loan charges are included by Peacock and Wiseman in their estimates
of expenditure on individual services. However, substantial amounts
of interest are in respect of housing revenue accounts which produce a
rental income, and advances for house purchase, which produce
payments of interest from mortgagors[1]; to show the interest payment
without the corresponding income would be misleading. The most
appropriate comparison is in terms of expenditure excluding debt
interest. Due to this and other differences of coverage, the figures
shown in the table for 1950 do not agree exactly with those in
Table 5.

The picture that emerges is of a rapid growth of local authorities'
expenditure, considerably faster relative to GNP than before World
War II, and especially rapid in the 1960s. Changes in housing policy
caused considerable shifts in the rate of rise of local authorities'
expenditure, both as a proportion of GNP and as a proportion of
total expenditure; but if attention is confined to services other than
housing, local authorities' expenditure still tended to rise somewhat
more rapidly than expenditure by the Central government. Com-
parisons in the 1950–55 period are liable to convey a misleading

[1] Of total interest paid in respect of rate-fund services in England and Wales in
1967/68 of £551·7m., £318·4m. (58%) was in respect of Housing Revenue
Accounts, and £56·5m. (10%) was in respect of advances under the Housing
Acts. *Local Government Financial Statistics*, 1967/68, Table I.

Table 6: *Central and Local Government Expenditure in relation to GNP, 1950–68*

	1950	1955	1960	1968
Total Expenditure		(% of GNP)		
Central Government	29·2	27·2	25·9	28·6
Local Authorities	9·6	10·4	10·5	15·7
Domestic Civil Expenditure				
Central Government	16·4	13·8	15·2	19·6
Local Authorities	8·9	9·4	9·3	13·3
Domestic Civil Expenditure Excluding Housing				
Central Government	15·9	13·2	14·7	20·0
Local Authorities	6·3	6·8	7·6	10·7
Expenditure by Local Authorities	(% of Total Public Expenditure)			
All Expenditure	24·8	27·6	29·0	34·7
Domestic Civil Expenditure	35·2	40·6	37·8	40·0
Domestic Civil Expenditure excluding Housing	28·5	33·7	34·3	35·1

Source: Calculated from expenditure series derived from *National Income and Expenditure*, 1969, Tables 1, 38, 39, 42, 43, 45 and 50; and corresponding tables in earlier years.

impression, because the total of Central government expenditure was held down by once-and-for-all reductions in food subsidies.

The Growth of Local Authorities' Expenditure 1950-67

The rates of growth of expenditure shown in Table 6 were in terms of percentages of GNP. This measure has value, for GNP is a useful indicator of scale; but by itself it can be misleading, in that the rate of increase of GNP itself is variable over time. In this section of the paper, attention will be concentrated on the rate of growth of local authorities' expenditure in absolute terms, and an attempt made to sub-divide the total increase in expenditure into growth in real terms, the rise in the general level of prices, and the rise in the 'price' of local authority services in relation to the general level of prices. This analysis is most appropriately made in respect of expenditure excuding housing, since swings in expenditure on housing have been so large and rapid as to obscure trends in expenditure on the other local authority services, where the rate of increase has tended to alter much more gradually.

Public expenditure on house building rose rapidly in the early 1950s, by over 30% (at constant prices) between 1950 and 1953. It then declined steeply in the next four years or so, and more gradually after that, as local authorities' programmes were cut back partly for reasons of economic management and partly to make way for an expansion of building for sale to private owners. In the early 1960s policies changed again; it was evident that in the large urban areas housing shortages and concentrations of poor housing persisted, and that these could not be tackled by building for sale. Between 1961 and 1967 investment in new housing by the public sector more than doubled. Not all of this increase was due to the larger number of houses built; standards were raised, and the proportion of flats in expensive high-rise blocks increased. The course of new house building by the public sector is summarised in Table 7. It includes houses built by public authorities for their own personnel (e.g. married quarters for the armed forces) but this element is too small to make the picture unrepresentative of local authorities and new towns.

Table 7: *House Building by the Public Sector,* 1950–68

	Dwellings Started (thousands)	Dwellings Completed (thousands)	Gross fixed Capital Formation (£m. at 1958 prices)
1950	188·8	175·2	395(a)
1953	270·0	255·9	519
1957	153·4	174·6	317
1961	127·1	122·4	286
1964	184·7	161·9	462
1967	222·5	211·2	611
1968	201·2	199·8	654(b)

Note:

(a) Approximate estimate only, due to revaluation from 1954 to 1958 prices.
(b) Approximate estimate only, due to revaluation from 1963 prices to 1968 prices.

Sources: Dwellings started and completed: 1950, *Monthly Digest of Statistics,* September 1954, Table 88; 1953 and subsequent years, *Housing Statistics,* No. 15, Table 2. Gross fixed capital formation: *National Income and Expenditure,* 1969, Table 51; and corresponding table in earlier years.

Lending by local authorities for house purchase has also fluctuated sharply, and in the 1960s accounts for a considerable part of the year to year variation, in housing expenditure. Net lending rose from £59m. in 1963 to £169m. in 1965[1] and then, following the imposition in July 1965 of a limit to total gross new lending, fell back to £44m. in 1966 and to minus £3m. in 1968. Local authorities' expenditure on housing is a large proportion of their total expenditure; it was 33% (excluding debt interest) in 1953, the highest proportion ever, and 22% in 1967; but the swings in it can readily be traced to specific changes in policy, so that in analysing the factors accounting for the growth of local authorities' expenditure it is proper to concentrate on total expenditure excluding housing.

In Table 8 below an analysis is made of the rise in total expenditure other than housing, to sub-divide it into (a) the increase in expenditure in real terms; (b) the effect of rise in the general level of prices, and (c) the increase in the price of local authority services in relation to the general level of prices. GNP at current and constant prices are shown for comparison. The analysis is an approximate one only, since revaluation at constant prices poses very difficult problems.[2]

By every measure there was a sharp acceleration in the average rate of increase in local expenditure between 1955–60 and 1960–67; and in terms of costs specific to local government (i.e. excluding the rise in the general price level[3] the rate of increase was appreciably more rapid in 1955–60 than in 1950–55. The increase in expenditure at constant prices was extremely rapid over the period 1960–67; the rise in the relative price of local authority expenditure was slower than in the previous period, in part because a larger proportion of the increase consisted of capital expenditure, where the relative price increase was much less than for current expenditure on goods and services.

[1] *National Income and Expenditure*, 1968, Table 46.

[2] For current expenditure on goods and services, reliance is placed on the implicit deflators derived from the constant price series published in Table 14 of *National Income and Expenditure*, 1969. For gross fixed capital formation, the implicit deflators for 'social services' and 'other public services' derived from Tables 55 and 56 of *National Income and Expenditure*, 1969 (and corresponding tables for earlier years). For current grants to persons, the Index of Retail Prices and, before 1956, the Interim Index were used for revaluation.

[3] The measure used in the index of the price of 'all final goods and services sold on the home market'. *National Income and Expenditure*, 1969, Table 16.

Table 8: *Components of Growth of Local Authorities'*
Expenditure other than Housing, 1950–68

	(*Annual averages % a year*)		
	1950–55	1955–60	1960–68
Increase in expenditure in real terms	2·8	3·5	6·2
Rise in general price level	4·8	2·8	3·5
Rise in relative price level of local authority expenditure	1·2	2·1	1·0
Total increase in expenditure in money terms	9·0	8·7	10·9
Increase in GNP at current prices	7·7	6·0	6·1
Increase in GNP at constant prices	2·7	2·5	2·9

Sources: See text for local authorities' expenditure at current and constant prices. GNP and general price level from *National Income and Expenditure*, 1969, Tables 1, 14 and 16.

The Composition of the Increase in Local Authorities' Expenditure

The next step is to examine the composition of the increase in local authorities' expenditure. This part of the analysis must be in terms of current prices, as there is insufficient information about prices for estimates to be good for each service in terms of constant prices. Table 9 shows the absolute increases in expenditure between 1955 and 1960, and 1960 and 1968; the increase in expenditure on each service as a proportion of the total increase; and the annual average increase. No analysis is made for the increase between 1950 and 1955 because of changes in the classification of expenditure.

Several features stand out from the table, notably the continued rapid growth of expenditure on education throughout the period; the much faster increase in expenditure on health and welfare services and child care in the second period than in the first; the rapid increase in the second period in expenditure on roads; the very large increase after 1960 in expenditure on police and fire services; and the very large increase in expenditure between 1960 and 1968 on 'other services'. This item includes expenditure on urban redevelopment (other than housing). Redevelopment schemes in the early 1960s are a major reason for the very rapid increase in expenditure.

Table 9: *Increase in Local Authorities' Expenditure, 1955–68, by Category of Service*

	1955–60			1960–68		
	Increase (£m.)	*Increase as % of Total*	*Annual Average Increase*	*Increase (£m.)*	*Increase as % of Total*	*Annual Average Increase*
Education (a)	331	55·5	10·0	1,069	47·1	10·5
Health and Welfare	34	5·7	6·8	156	6·9	11·7
Child Care	5	4·8	4·4	34	1·5	11·7
Roads and Public Lighting (b)	62	10·4	8·7	229	10·1	10·7
Sewerage and Refuse Disposal	64	10·7	12·0	186	8·2	11·8
Water Supply (c)	6	1·0	3·4	27	1·2	6·8
Police	36	6·0	7·1	167	7·4	11·3
Fire Services	10	1·7	7·4	38	1·7	10·0
Parks, Pleasure Grounds, etc.	14	2·3	9·0	37	1·7	8·6
Libraries, Museums, and Arts	9	1·5	10·4	37	1·7	12·7
Trading Services (c)	10	1·7	8·8	41	1·8	11·6
Other Services	15	2·5	2·3	246	10·8	12·9
All Services other than Housing	*596*	*100·0*	*8·7*	*2,267*	*100·0*	*11·0*

Notes: (a) Includes school meals and milk;
(b) Includes car parks;
(c) Capital expenditure only.

Source: Calculated from *National Income and Expenditure*, 1966, Tables 45 and 46; and 1969, Tables 42 and 43.

It is not possible here to comment in any detail on the development of the individual services, but a few prominent features may be highlighted. Provision for an increasing urban and suburban population, spread over a wider area, has necessitated substantial increases in investment in water supply and sewerage and sewage disposal, and refuse collection and disposal. Technical circumstances, e.g. the need to go further afield for water supplies, and the increasing shortage of suitable sites for disposing of refuse are tending to raise costs. The growing volume of traffic has made necessary much enlarged expenditure on urban roads, and has been a contributing reason for the increase in expenditure on police services. The average increase of over 11% a year in the cost of police services is testimony to the demands made for additional resources to cope with the rise in crime and the growth of traffic. Provision of basic services for a growing population is a major reason for the rapid growth of local authorities' expenditure.

The expansion of local authorities' expenditure on education is well known and has been much discussed. But there has been rather less comment on the expansion of local health and welfare services. The 1959 Mental Health Act laid on county boroughs and counties a duty to provide care for the mentally ill and handicapped who were not hospital in-patients. How exactly the role of 'community care' in this field will develop is still uncertain; but it is probable that the trend towards greater reliance on out-patient or short-stay in-patient treatment for mental illness will lead to demands for a much enlarged provision for mental illness by the local health services. Similarly, the trend towards reducing the length of stay in hospital for other kinds of illness is increasing the demands on the local health services. The services provided by the local health and welfare services have expanded substantially in the 1960s; but there is no lack of pressure for further improvements.

The proportion of the increase in local authorities' expenditure that is attributable to 'civic amenities', to use Professor Hicks's term[1], is small. Even if all of the increase in expenditure on libraries and museums, parks, and 'other services' (which include urban redevelopment and new local authority offices) are regarded as attributable to civic amenities, they account for only 14% of the total increase in expenditure (other than on housing) between 1960 and 1968; of the increase in expenditure other than education, their share was 27%.

[1] See p. 159 above.

The principal reasons for the growth of local authorities' expenditure have been the development of education; expansion of health and welfare services; and provision of the environmental services required by a growing population of which an increasing proportion own cars.

Local Authorities' Expenditure and the Management of the Economy

Local authorities' expenditure is a very substantial part of the demand on the economy; in 1968 their direct expenditure on goods and services and gross fixed capital formation was equal to one-eighth of GNP, and they accounted for between one-fifth and one-quarter of all gross fixed capital formation. At mid-1968, just over 9% of the total working population in employment were employed by local authorities; between 1958 and 1968, the number of people employed by local authorities rose by 650,000, equal to 64% of the total increase in the employed working population[1]. Since local authorities collectively make so substantial a claim on the resources of the economy, there is little scope for excluding them from the exigencies of economic management.

Moreover, when reductions in public expenditure are needed for reasons of economic control, as in early 1968, there is no real possibility of all of the reductions in expenditure falling on direct expenditure by the Central government. To secure reductions in planned expenditure of the size needed for controlling the level of demand on the economy, recourse has to be had to reductions in local authorities' expenditure. This has its problems for economic management, quite apart from the efficient development of local services. Local authorities are numerous[2]; because of their number, information about their expenditure even in total is less accurate and up-to-date than about Central government expenditure, and there is more uncertainty about how their expenditure, given a continuation of present policies, will move over the next year or so. The Central government's powers to control or influence local expenditure through loan sanctions or the rate support grant are not well fitted for using local authorities' expenditure for managing the economy.

[1] *National Income and Expenditure*, 1969, Table 13.

[2] As at March 1969 there were 1,425 counties, boroughs, and county districts in England and Wales, and 234 cities, counties and burghs in Scotland.

The disadvantages of using short-term variations in public expenditure as a means of regulating the economy are well-known and widely commented on; but given public attitudes to taxation and the limits to which private investment can be cut without impairing economic growth, it has proved impossible to eschew cuts in public expenditure. In this respect, the growth of local authorities' expenditure compared with direct expenditure by the Central government makes the latter's problems of managing the economy all the greater.

Future Prospects for Local Authorities' Expenditure

To assert that local authorities' expenditure cannot continue to grow at the rate recently experienced is but to state a truism. Table 6 above shows that local authorities' expenditure, excluding debt interest, rose from 9·4% of GNP in 1960 to 13·3% of GNP in 1968, i.e. by an average of 0·5% of GNP a year. If this rate were to continue, then in about seventy years' time one-half of GNP would consist of local government services. This is clearly an example of unjustified extrapolation; but to point to its absurdity does not help in making an assessment of what is likely to be the course of local authorities' expenditure in the next ten to fifteen years.

In some respects, the early and middle 1960s can be seen to have been a period when the growth of local authority expenditure was quite exceptionally rapid. The reduction in the housing programme made by the Government early in 1968 checked the rise in local authorities' capital expenditure on housing; and in the longer term a further rise in the number of houses built by local authorities on the scale experienced between 1961 and 1967 is most improbable, as the stock of houses is growing considerably faster, at present rates of building, than the number of households. But apart from housing, pressures for expansion of local authority services are likely to remain strong. Education is an expanding service; during the 1970s the growth of the secondary school population will be especially rapid, due to demographic change, raising the school-leaving age, and the probable continuation of the trend towards voluntary later leaving. The circumstances that led to the expansion of the local health and welfare services are likely to persist for a long time to come. Increases in the population and in the number of dwellings and households, to say nothing of growing concern about pollution, are likely to bring about substantial increases in demands on the environmental services. The continuing growth of the volume of traffic will lead to continuing pressure for higher expenditure on urban road schemes. What the outcome of these pressures will be, both in terms of the balance between rates of growth of the main services and in terms of the share of total national resources devoted to local government services, will depend on decisions taken by local authorities and the Central government have to try to reconcile the probably irreconcilable wishes of the electorate in their capacity as users of public services and their capacity as tax- and rate-payers.

Index